IN THE
Treasures from the Dark
MIDST

JOHN STUMBO

Nesting Tree
BOOKS

Published by Nesting Tree Books
Cover Design: Matt DeCoste
Interior Design: Deborah Schermerhorn
Editor: Sue Miholer
Proofreading: Rebecca Anderson
Cover Photo: flickr.com/photos/clickr-bee
Author Photo: Daron Short

ISBN: 978-0-9839333-1-1

Printed in the United States of America.

*To the praying people of Salem Alliance Church
and the thousands of others around the world
who wouldn't let go of heaven
until heaven let go of me.*

*To my friend, Robb,
who launched the blog
that launched this book.*

*To the blog community
who believed I still had something to say
even when I had no voice to say it.*

*To Joanna,
my cherished wife,
whose whole life is vivid evidence
that a God of love walks with us
even on the most complicated trails.*

*And,
to all those who have entered the fellowship of the suffering,
still believing
that some of God's richest treasures
are preserved in the darkest places.*

Powerful Pictures 69
One Twig in the Family Tree–Parts 1 and 2 72
One Twig in the Family Tree–Part 3 (Conclusion) 74
Prayer-Worriers: Thought-Powered–Part 1 77
Inedible Dreams: Thought-Powered–Part 2 80
Getting Specific: Thought-Powered–Part 3 83
Thought-Powered–Conclusion 85
A Day at Sea 88
Quick Update 91
Tough and Tender Caregivers 92
He Made Me Proud 94
Verbs of Faith–Part 1 96
Verbs of Faith–Part 2 99
Verbs of Faith–Part 3 101
Verbs of Faith–Part 4 103
Verbs of Faith–A Poetic Postscript 105
Sequestered 108
In A Perfect World 110
A Good Pruning 112
Off-Road Faith 114
The Blog I Didn't Plan on Writing 116
One Shovel at a Time 118
Persevere-Hints–Part 1 120
Persevere-Hints–Part 2 124
Persevere-Hints–Part 3 (Genesis 39) 127
Clap Anyway 130
A Child's Cry: A Short Story 132
Who is Calling the Shots? 135
The Fine Art of Asking for Help 137
Patient Patients and Caring Caregivers 140
Glancing Over My Shoulder: Ranting–Part 1 143
Shoulder: Ranting–Part 2 146
Ranting–Conclusion 149

Year Two

The Setting..153
A Year Later–Part 1..155
A Year Later–Part 2..157
A Year Later–Part 3..160
A Year Later–Part 4..163
A Year Later–Part 5..165
A Year Later–Part 6..168
A Year Later–Conclusion..170
Tough Assignments..173
Going With the Flow..175
The Last Hour of the Year..177
TNTQ..179
Body and Spirit..181
A Word to Those Who Suffer..183
Of Dreams and Hopes and Flower Bulbs..185
A Declaration of Faith..187
The Question We're Really Asking..190
March Update..193
Where I'm Heading Changes How I'm Walking..195
The Friday We Call "Good"..197
Seeing Suffering by Candlelight..200
Reentry..204
Rejoice With Me..206
A Psalm of Praise..209
Baby Bites and Big Lessons..212
Test-Taking Tips..215
Saddle Up!..218
Expectations..219
It's Wednesday..221
On Snipers and Souls and Hard Days..223
Untangling–Part 1..225
Untangling–Part 2..227
Untangling–Conclusion..229
You: A Joyful Declaration of the Sovereignty of God..231
Strength Enough..233
Whew!..236
About Formulas, Faith and Life Change..238
In the Moment..241
My Seatmate..244

Year Three

The Setting...249
Joy From a Prison Cell..251
Packin' One Less Thing...254
Things Underthanked 257
Milk in the Fridge and Feet on the Ground...260
Behind the Scenes of the First Christmas ... and This One, Too 262
The Path of Healing: Ancient Lessons from the Diseased................265
Larger Souls–Part 1..269
Larger Souls–Part 2..272
Larger Souls–Conclusion...275
A Prayer for Humility on Palm Sunday...278
Praying Through Pain...280
A Prayer: One Week, Two Trees, Many Parallels..282
June Update..284
Finding Solace in Simple Truths...287
The Finish Line for Year Three 289

Conclusion

The Setting...297
Passing Through...298
Epilogue..301

INTRODUCTION

This is an odd book.

Most books are written by people who believe they have something to say, a story to tell or a contribution to make. We think of authors as "experts" or at least people who can speak *authoritatively* on a subject.

In contrast, this book is a compilation of writings from a guy who didn't feel like he had much to say, had no clue where his story was heading and wrote not so much to make a contribution, but for his personal survival. I should know. I'm the guy.

The prose, prayers and poems you will read were written in the midst of suffering. I don't use that word lightly, nor do I believe that my "suffering" compares to that of others. I've merely been to the minor leagues compared to some of you veteran "major leaguers" who've kept stepping up to the plate in spite of huge losses, chronic pain and the worst that a fallen world throws at us.

My crisis began on a fabulous October afternoon in Oregon. I had never spent a day in the hospital since birth. I had good genes, good habits, good health and a good outlook on life. I felt as secure as any 47-year-old has felt. To my great surprise, I would spend most of the next three months in the hospital and most of the next three years in various phases of recovery. It was during this long recovery that this book was written.

However, writing it wasn't my idea.

During the hospitalization, the leadership of our local church determined that the most effective way to keep people informed as to my condition was to post updates on the church website. This proved to be a very helpful tool to keep information accurate and rumors minimal. It also served to encourage much prayer.

When I was released, it was suggested that I take over writing the updates. The world of blogging had become popular and those around me suggested that this would be a good form of communication. I never had interest in writing or reading blogs, but I did see this as an opportunity to thank the thousands of people who were praying for us and to give them an occasional progress report. I greatly underestimated the significance of this decision. In the years that followed, I would write hundreds of posts that would be read by thousands of people. And, the writings now take the form of this book.

I've not included many of the day-to-day updates, i.e. the "newsy" stuff that seems less relevant now. Small adjustments were made to a few of the entries to give the book a sense of continuity. Other than that, there has been minimal editing in what you will read. These are raw, real-time writings. To make major changes to them would only make them less authentic.

For those who don't know my story, this book will be more meaningful if you also read *An Honest Look at a Mysterious Journey*. In it, my wife and I relive the story of recent years in a transparent manner.

Speaker and author, Ravi Zacharias kindly endorsed the book by saying, "You listen to a testimony like John Stumbo's and you cry because there are many things we will never understand. But we wipe away the tears because we know how a Sovereign God is able to even take the weak of this world to tell a story that will confound the wise. This is one of the most powerful stories that I have ever heard. It will change the way you face life's twists and turns."

But this book that you now hold was written *in the midst* of the making of the story. With feeding tube hanging from my stomach, wound vacuum attached to my leg and heaviness weighing my heart, I wrote. With no promise that I would be physically healed, I wrote. With every truth that I had ever preached being challenged, I wrote. Without expectation that my writings would ever be put into book form, I wrote. And, when sweet gifts of healing came, I continued to write.

Someone long ago said, "I didn't know what I believed until I wrote it down." On my sickbed, I had countless hours to think. Most of my thoughts felt quite unhelpful and often unhealthy. A battle raged inside my mind, and for many hours of the day I was losing the battle.

Writing—the laborious work of birthing words out of ideas and meaningful sentences out of those words—became a spiritual discipline of sorts. I submitted myself, at least a few times a week, to the discipline of putting paragraphs on a screen that I could believe and defend, even if only for a few moments. The raging storm of thoughts blowing recklessly through my head were lassoed and subdued as I wrote. A few of these writings were dictated by me and typed by my daughter since the very act of typing was grievous.

Some days, as dis-ease played havoc in my body and spirit, my own writings mocked me and gave cause for an even more sinister voice to taunt, "Didn't you just write about faith, or perseverance or prayer? What do you think of your words now? Hypocrite!"

Sometimes the best silencer of the taunting voice was to submit to the "discipline" yet once more and write again. *This I believe. This is the man I want to be. These are the truths to which I must cling.*

So, this is how this book came to be. I never set out to write it. I wondered and wandered. I grieved and grappled. I kept trying to find my footing and bearings on a precarious and foggy trail.

But now that more time has passed, I've become convinced that these writings must be shared. I'm humbled that you'd join me in the journey. I pray that where you find your own story intersecting with mine you'll receive comfort, wisdom and grace.

Respectfully,
John Stumbo—Age 51

PREAMBLE

I forgot I had written it.

As I assembled material for this book, I found the following poem buried in the soundless world of old computer files. I stumbled across it like an acquaintance I once knew but hadn't seen in years. I gasped so loudly when I rediscovered it that Joanna came in from the next room to ask if I was okay.

As I read it, the memory came back clearly.

It was a lovely August evening. Unknown to me, in just a few months I would be on my deathbed. I did not intend to write a poem that night. But, a prompting thought wandered through my brain about getting on a "poet's train." Sometimes when I write, I merely have a "seed" thought as I begin, having no idea about what the seed will become. I water it with a little reflection and see what it grows into. Such was the case with this poem. By the time I was done, I realized that my heart was chasing down the idea that I needed to not mimic other authors, but try to find my own voice.

—❧—

A Poet's Train

John Stumbo—Age 47

Once I boarded a poet's train
But had to write my own refrain.
He would not share his pen nor rhyme
And firmly swore that I find mine.

We made our way a-clicky-clack
Along the lonesome set of track.
My mind was all a-blicky-blink,
As I found it too hard to think.

I hummed a tune, I said a prayer,
I ran my fingers through my hair.
I strolled, I paced, I got a drink,
I took a nap, just for a wink.

When I had picked that poet's train,
I got on board to pick his brain.
But one must write from his own heart;
There is no other place to start.

I pulled the cord, the train did slow,
I bid farewell, for now I know
If I'm to write a song or tale
It must be found on my own trail.

Once I boarded a poet's train
But had to write my own refrain.
And now I'm glad he would not share
For my own heart was not found there.

Sometimes we write not for the crowd;
We dare not even read aloud.
We write that we might know ourselves
To learn the depths our spirit delves.

To ride the heights our thoughts do soar
To understand what's in our core.
To find the secrets here within
To feel that that we're alive again.

I'm grateful for that poet's train
But I won't come this way again.
A lonely trail is my best choice
To hear my heart, to find my voice.

———

I had no idea how lonely that trail would be.

The night I wrote this poem, I had a romanticized picture of that "lonely trail." I'd fill a backpack with a healthy lunch, a little chocolate, plenty of water, a Bible, a couple of good pens and a notebook. I'd hike for miles, enjoying the sweetness of God in His creation. Eventually I'd find a gentle stream and a log that had long ago fallen just to give me a place to sit, listen and write. I could spend all day in this place—emotionally still, physically strong, spiritually alive.

The poem proved to be oddly prophetic. I *would* find a lonely trail upon which I would find my voice. It just wasn't the trail I anticipated. Rather than long, robust hikes along shaded streams, my lonely trail took me to the sequestered confines of a wheelchair. My days would be spent, not in a vast forest, but in the few hundred square feet of a few rooms of our house.

Unexpected though it bc, I would find my trail and, yes, with it I would find my voice.

Year One

I will give you the treasures of darkness,
Riches stored in secret places,
So that you may know that I am the Lord,
The God of Israel, who summons you by name.

Isaiah 45:3 (NIV 1984)

THE SETTING

After seventy-seven days of hospitalization, I was allowed to return home. A mysterious condition had devoured my muscular system, causing me to lose fifty pounds, primarily of muscle mass. I was left with profound muscle weakness from my face to my feet. The site of the tracheotomy incision was healing nicely, but an infected muscle biopsy in my right thigh was not. I could shuffle around the house with the aid of a walker, but any trip, such as to a doctor's office, required a wheelchair. And, since my arms were too weak to push the chair more than a few feet, I needed continual assistance. The feeding tube hanging from my stomach was the only way for hydration, medication and nutrition to enter my body since my swallow had completely ceased to function. I lived with spit rags and paper towels to capture my saliva. I slept fifteen hours a day and had very little energy the other nine.

In other words, I was a mess.

But, I was home and I had hope . . . at least at first. I was confident that whatever had about killed me was now receding and that it was only a matter of time and I'd once again be healthy enough to resume my role as lead pastor of our church.

I had hope, I had confidence, and I had a community of people praying for me.

In my first posting I wrote, "My intent is to update this page a couple times a week. I'll use this space to fill you in on my health condition, but I also intend to use this as an opportunity to explore what has been going on in my heart during this mind-boggling journey. Writing helps me sort out my thoughts. I pray that these thoughts will have some value for you as well."

Two days later I would add, "Emotionally, Joanna and I are holding together pretty well. We have our moments of gloom and/or tears, but most of our days are marked by peace or at least acceptance. We are convinced that God has us in this sequestered place at this time, so we'll attempt to keep trusting Him. I'll be sharing some of my 'wrestlings,' questions and lessons in later blogs."

In the months that followed, these "wrestlings" became more intense. All evidence indicated that I was not improving physically and my emotional strength—like an athlete clinging to the chin-up bar—could only hold out for so long. As the year progressed, I would question matters of faith and battle with discouragement and depression. For months, I would experience what the saints of old have called the "dark night of the soul."

My hope and confidence would wane, but the support of the community did not. I remain grateful to them to this day.

February 13
MY VALENTINE:
KUDOS TO CAREGIVERS

I have a great blessing: My nurse is my Valentine.

Who knew twenty-six years ago that I married the world's greatest nurse? Okay, she doesn't do blood very well, but other than that Joanna is an amazing caregiver. Countless times a day she responds to my needs: greasing my parched skin, getting me dressed, helping me shower, getting me to appointments, maneuvering my wheelchair, clearing a path for my walker, turning things on and off that I can't reach, grinding my medications so they can be put into liquid form for the feeding tube, opening the cans of "medical food" and pouring them into my feeding tube four times a day, picking up after me, giving me words and hugs of encouragement—and on the list goes. All this without a word of complaint. She claims she's pleased to do it—amazing. My wife, the no-complaint saint.

Meanwhile, I know that many of you are involved in caregiving of some type as well. A portion or even the entirety of your day is dedicated to the well-being of another person: parents of young children, spouses of invalids, those in the helping professions, friends who go out of their way to help someone do what they cannot do for themselves . . . on the list goes. I celebrate you today.

As caregivers, you may have the tendency to deflect my words at this moment. You are so accustomed to giving that you may have a weakness in receiving. Please pause and receive these words as a message to you.

To you, the New Testament declares, "God is not unjust; he will not forget your work and the love you have shown him as you have helped his people and continue to help them" (Hebrews 6:10). I love the insight into the character of God that this verse reveals: God so closely identifies with people in need that when you care for one of them, He takes it personally. You show love to Him as you lovingly care for those assigned to you. You may have thought you were just blessing one person—you are actually blessing God Himself. Stunning.

And as you do, you reflect Christ well—the Christ who said of Himself: "The Son of Man did not come to be served, but to serve, and to give his life as a ransom for many" (Matthew 20:28).

So, to all the caregivers, I celebrate you today. You have a high calling. You are a gift to those of us in need. God isn't going to forget the work you have done. He considers that it would be an act of injustice if He did. And, though we may not always express our gratitude well, those of us on the receiving end are the better because of you. Thank you.

Blessed are the caregivers, for they have touched the heart of God.

February 19
VIEWS

I lost count, but I think I was in at least nine different hospital rooms during my seventy-seven-day adventure.

Typically my bed faced the door and/or a whiteboard telling me the date and my nurse's name. Occasionally, however, the nurses would turn my bed in such a way that I could look out the window. As I grew stronger and the nurses propped me up in a chair, I'd always ask for a window view. In my first hospital, it seems that I usually had a corner room, which meant I had the view of an exterior wall on the other side of the building. Gratefully, someone had planned ahead and planted a tree in the space in between so at least I had some green to appreciate. During my long stay in an intensive care unit in Portland, Oregon, I had an incredible view of the city and (on a clear day) the mountains. However, I was too sick to really enjoy the scene—especially since most of this occurred during an extended snowstorm. The dreary gray of the sky matched my spirit at the time.

My third place of hospitalization was at a rehabilitation center. My window looked directly at the state hospital—a cool building, but not exactly a place that inspires.

But during these seventy-seven days of hospitalization, my favorite view was when I was able to look down over the hospital's front entrance. Here life was happening, people were coming and going, and—of greatest interest to me—an occasional jogger would pass. I assumed they were on their way to the bark-dust trail of city park just blocks away—a trail I've pounded dozens of times myself. Watching them jog past stirred up mixed emotions within me: pleasure in seeing someone doing something I love and a sad reminder of my incapacitated condition. My window view forced me to think about my own view of my situation.

Meanwhile, I received cards, emails and blog comments from so many of you. Thank you. One of them came from a longtime friend of the family who is a pastor's wife in the Midwest. Her family had recently experienced a difficult transition. In a letter to me she shared a portion of her journal arising from this time of tough adjustment. She felt like she had far more in the "loss" column than in the "win" one. As she closed her journal entry she included a prayer. I believe it is full of wisdom. She prayed, "God, give me a heart of *gratitude* for what was, a heart of *acceptance* for what is and a heart of *anticipation* for what is to come."

I love this prayer. I must confess, however, that I can easily fall into a completely different mind-set. Gratitude, acceptance and anticipation don't always come naturally. My attitude can become one of being *forlorn* about the past, *frustrated* about the present and *fearful* of the future: forlorn because I so badly miss aspects of my prior life, frustrated because I'm sick of being sick and fearful that I may not ever return to 100% capacity. This, obviously, is not a good way to live, but "soul gravity" tries to pull me in that direction.

As I've grown stronger physically, I can now choose my own window view. I can shuffle my walker, pull up a shade and look out any window I choose. A strengthened soul can do the same. May each of us today choose the best view in the "house."

February 21
OXYMORONS

Oxymorons. You remember what they are: two words that appear contradictory like *known secret*. Or how about these: *reality TV, sad smile, humane killer, jumbo shrimp, deeply shallow, buffalo wings, climb down, civil war, same difference* or *dead livestock*. I find it interesting that the word "oxymoron" comes from two Greek words: *oxy* (meaning "sharp" or "pointed") and *moros* (meaning "dull"). So you can see that the word "oxymoron" is itself an oxymoron.

One oxymoron that has arisen in my world lately is "bed exercises." Many of the good folks in physical therapy are accustomed to working with people who spend most of their days in bed; thus they have devised exercises especially suited for being flat on your back. These are all helpful and good, I'm sure. I just have one problem with the scenario: When I go to bed, I'm thinking about going to sleep, not doing sets of ten leg lifts!

I've enjoyed reading through Jeremiah for my morning devotions this month. Jeremiah has a difficult life assignment: As one author summarizes, "Jeremiah was called by God to the unhappy task of telling an unheeding nation it was going to be judged and destroyed."

As he faithfully fulfills this calling, one of the gifts Jeremiah gives us is that he is more autobiographical than any of the other prophets. He provides an inside look into his life and emotions.

He's very open about:

- His *passion*, "Your words are what sustain me. They bring me great joy and are my heart's delight" (15:16, NLT);

- His *frustration,* "O Hope of Israel, our Savior in times of trouble! Why are you like a stranger to us? Why are you like someone passing through the land, stopping only for the night?" (14:8, NLT);

- His *grief,* "Oh, that my eyes were a fountain of tears; I would weep forever!" (9:1, NLT);

- And his *faith,* "O Sovereign LORD! You have made the heavens and earth by your great power. Nothing is too hard for you!" (32:17, NLT).

Meanwhile, he fills us in on numerous fascinating details of his life such as being thrown into a cistern and preaching with a yoke around his neck.

One of the most intriguing passages in Jeremiah feels like an oxymoron to me—two statements Jeremiah makes right next to each other that seem contradictory.

He writes with confidence: "The LORD stands beside me like a great warrior. Before him they will stumble. They cannot defeat me . . . I have committed my cause to you. Now I will sing out my thanks to the LORD!" (20:11–13, NLT).

Then, immediately, he shifts to this: "Yet I curse the day I was born! May the day of my birth not be blessed. I curse the messenger who told my father, 'Good news—you have a son!' . . . Oh, that I had died in my mother's womb, that her body had been my grave! Why was I ever born?" (20:14-18, NLT).

What is up with that? He's saying, "I'm singing praise to the Lord, my great warrior; but I really wish I were dead." What can we say about Jeremiah's wildly ranging statements?

First of all, he is honest. Jeremiah is a model of authenticity. Next, his statement reveals to us how safe Jeremiah felt as he talked with God. Third, although we may imagine that "transparency" is a recent concept from a counselor's office, Jeremiah models it from 600 BC. It's nothing new; it's just too rare.

Fourth, his statements suggest that two contradictory emotions are possible simultaneously in the human heart. Some of us know what this is like. Two contradictory streams merge. Both real. Both powerful. Finally, notice that Jeremiah doesn't resolve the tension—he doesn't undo the contradiction—he doesn't feel a need to wrap it all in a bow. He lets the oxymoron of his present condition hang there unsettled.

Today he gives me permission to do so as well.

ℳarch 2
A SIX-NOTE RANGE

Prior to this illness, I never knew how much of my personal identity was tied to my voice—as in literal vocal cords and sound. The ways I spoke, preached, sang, laughed, whispered—even coughed, burped and sneezed—were all part of this thing called "me." For a lifetime I heard myself a certain way and was quite comfortable with it.

Then they slit my throat—performed a tracheotomy—and I couldn't speak for weeks. Meanwhile, the muscle-attacking disease that had hammered other parts of my body found its way to my vocal cords and soft palate. The result is that I have a very weak and airy voice with not enough vocal-cord power and too much air coming out my nose rather than my mouth. "B's" and "p's" and "s's" are especially tough. I slur a lot of my words. I don't know what I sound like to you, but to me I sound like an old man with a bad sinus infection, who has smoked three packs a day for a lifetime and has been tipping the bottle all afternoon. I'm embarrassed by it. I used to love to sing—now I have a raspy six-note range. I'm not impressed.

The ever-encouraging wife of mine assures me that she likes my voice just as it is. I don't believe her until she pulls out her next line: "For a while, I didn't think I'd ever hear you speak again. So I'm happy with your voice however it sounds." What a great wife.

Since getting out of the hospital, this encouraging wife and I have been doing something we never really had the opportunity to do when I was a lead pastor: We've been attending church together. I cry every time I'm there. Last week's service closed with a very worshipful rendition of "I Love You, Lord." The song concludes, "Take joy, my King, in what You hear. May it be a sweet, sweet sound in Your ear."

I was drawn into worship and was attempting to sing the few notes that were in my range, but I was also thinking, *Take joy? Sweet, sweet sound? Hardly! Not from these vocal cords.* But at that moment I received a simple, quiet and gentle reassurance from the Father that it was indeed a sweet sound to Him. He doesn't evaluate music on the quality of the voice but on the condition of the heart. I may sound like a half-drunk emphysema victim, but my heart can be right and my worship sincere.

One day God gave Jeremiah a message to give to King Jehoiakim—an ungodly king who was building a marvelous palace but was using unjust labor practices in the process. Jeremiah warned him, "A beautiful palace does not make a great king!" (Jeremiah 22:15, NLT). May I paraphrase and say, "A beautiful voice does not make a great worshiper." God has a gazillion angels that can sing better than any voice on earth. He doesn't need more sound, but He *is* looking for more hearts.

Two applications: First, go to church this next weekend and offer what you've got. Quit holding back. Move from spectator to participant. Quit watching a show and join a celebration. Enter in. So you sound like Donald Duck and clap offbeat. You're not trying out for *American Idol;* you are giving back to God an offering of what He has given to you. He's the one who gave you that voice anyway. And be assured, He likes it—because it is yours, uniquely yours.

All that being said about voice and singing aside, I'm really trying to make a larger point. The greater application to my little singing experience is clearly this: What point of weakness in your life causes you to pull back from God? We all have some part of our life, experience, body, personality, etc., that we don't like. It is at this point that many of us cower from the Father. We feel more comfortable offering Him our strengths—*I can do this for You, Lord*—but to offer Him our places of embarrassment is more difficult. That place feels so broken, so unusable, so inappropriate to give. It seems like re-gifting a $25 gift card after you've used $17.99 of it.

Nevertheless, I assure you, that He is the God of cracked voices and cracked pots. He wants all of us. Quit holding out on Him. Offer Him what you have—weaknesses and all.

Okay, sermon ended. Care to join me in a song? I'll sing if you will.

I love You, Lord
And I lift my voice
To worship You
Oh, my soul rejoice!
Take joy my King
In what You hear
Let it be a sweet, sweet sound
In Your ear.

Words and music by Laurie Klein
© Universal Music Publishing Group

MOORINGS

I've promised you an honest look at my journey. Today's thoughts are an effort to keep that promise.

During my weeks in the intensive care unit, what I feared the most wasn't death. In fact, death seemed more like a friend than an enemy. Death would have been a great relief from what I was suffering. What I feared most wasn't my physical disability—although for a while I was very afraid that I would permanently be a quadriplegic.

During the worst days of my long stay in ICU, what I feared most was losing my mind. I truly thought—and deeply feared—that I was going insane. Looking back, I now understand that very high doses of medications were causing hallucinations and delusional thinking. However, I didn't know this at the time. All I knew was that it felt like I was going crazy. This condition lasted with intensity for about five days, with remnants lingering for a few more weeks.

The power and recurrence of some of the hallucinations were almost overwhelming. A month later I was still able to list over a dozen significant hallucinations I had experienced. Just last night I woke up at 3:00 a.m. remembering yet another one—dark and disturbing. The same emotions from ten weeks ago tried to sweep over me.

Some of the delusions were humorous; more were horrific. All of them were so very real. They were detailed, colorful, recurring, long, emotionally intense, vivid and again, oh so real.

In my confused state, I developed a method of fighting back mentally. I devised a little logic pattern of sorts. Looking back it wasn't all that logical, but at the time it made sense, and I returned to it often. I would rehearse in my head, "If _____ happens, then _____ will happen. If that happens, then _____ will happen." This progression went on for some length, the blanks being filled in by different scenarios depending on what I believed I was dealing with at the time—real or, more likely, delusional. The one part of the pattern that did not change was the final line. "And if _____ happens and I die, *I know I'm going to see Jesus.*" This one thought of seeing Jesus would pull me out of my panic, and a sense of stability and safety would guard my heart again.

I guess I found great solace in knowing that no matter how cruddy the journey might be, it had an incredible ending. The road may be rugged, but the final destination was assured and unbelievably good. *Even if the worst happens, I'll be with Jesus!*

These thoughts grounded me in a very unsettling time. The confidence that my current state, as horrific as it felt, would not go on forever is what kept hope alive.

I share this with you to celebrate that "we have this hope as an anchor for the soul, firm and secure" (Hebrews 6:19). Affixed to Christ, I am secure. Never in my life did this mean as much to me as when I was at my lowest.

I am so grateful for the assurance of salvation. As with all, I am so undeserving; yet I know that grace has been extended to me, my sins have been forgiven by the kindness and provision of Christ, and a place is being prepared for me in heaven.

I am assuming that most people reading these words share the same grateful assurance. But if you do not have a relationship with Christ, do not let another sun set before you have a serious conversation with God. Open a Bible to the third chapter of the Gospel of John and discover the relationship that Jesus wants to have with you. Include a Christian friend if you have one. Or, contact an evangelical pastor and explain your desire for a relationship with Christ. Begin a journey that leads all the way to heaven.

Without life-giving faith, you lack an anchor for your soul. Adrift, you are grasping for some stability. Christ is God's solution for the floundering soul, Christ is our hope. Christ is our anchor. Turn to Him.

God has given us eternal life, and this life is in his Son.
Whoever has the Son has life;
whoever does not have the Son of God does not have life.
I write these things to you who believe in the name of the Son of God
so that you may know that you have eternal life.

1 John 5:11–13

March 11
THE DANCE

I know poetry isn't everyone's favorite. And I don't claim to be a poet. However, I do find real value on occasion from this type of communication. It tends to take the mind and soul to places otherwise unexplored.

Below you will find an expression of my heart—an invitation to the Holy Spirit.

Dance upon my window
Dance upon my soul
Dance throughout my spirit
Come to make me whole.

Darkness stalks about me
Weakness lurks within
Sadness lies in shadows
Wearing resolve thin.

Holiness holds position
Forgiveness stands in place
Passion still arises
Calling out for grace.

Come, Delightful Healer
Come, Mysterious Dove
Come, Maker of Music
Dance Your song of love.

—⟨∞⟩—

I will pour out my Spirit on all people.
Your sons and daughters will prophesy,
Your old men will dream dreams,
Your young men will see visions.
Even on my servants, both men and women,
I will pour out my Spirit in those days.
Joel 2:28–29

The LORD your God is with you,
The Mighty Warrior who saves.
He will take great delight in you;
In his love he will no longer rebuke you,
But will rejoice over you with singing.
Zephaniah 3:17

March 13
BLOG CLOG

Like a sink with a hairball in the drain, not much is passing through my brain these days . . . at least not much worthy of recording. I haven't felt very good and my thinking has been sludgy.

I share this with you for two reasons. One, I want to let you know that I am in a recovery stage where I have some days that are far better than others. And, two, to let you know to not bother checking in on this blog for a few days. Hopefully by then the inspiration, energy and clarity will return. I love doing this blog. It has been a great encouragement to me in my journey—to have a reason to gather together my own meandering thoughts and to have you interact with them. So, I'll be back—happily—but until then, like the old country song says, "If the Phone Don't Ring, Baby, You'll Know It's Me."

With love and perseverance,
John

P.S. Don't worry about me. The very fact that I am posting this little piece is evidence that the hairball is dissolving.

March 16
WRITING FROM THE MIDDLE: JACOB–PART 1

Four times a day Joanna assists me with my tube feeding. This is a very unglamorous twenty minutes of pouring liquefied medicines and cans of soybean, corn and oat mixture through a tube directly into my stomach. Once a day, you'll find us doing so by our laptop computer while reading your latest blog comments—which we are very grateful for. They've caused us to laugh, cry, reminisce, reflect and appreciate.

One encouraging comment came from a woman we have never met: "God is using your words in a profound way," she claims. "You are speaking in the middle of the storm and we need to hear what you have to say."

Well, I'm not convinced my words are "needed," but I appreciate the insight that I'm writing from the "middle." I currently have no way of knowing where this journey leads or how long it lasts. Some praying people have said to me that they are believing for my full recovery. I hope they are right. I, personally, haven't heard from the Lord on this matter. What I do see are confused doctors, physical limitations and mental/emotional/spiritual battles. (How does one separate the body, psyche and spirit?)

Yes, my new friend, I am definitely writing from the "middle." She refers to it as the "middle of a storm." Joanna has used the metaphor of a tunnel. We know how long we've been in it, but we see no light yet at the end or have any way of knowing if we're 10% or 90% through it. We hope we're somewhere in the middle. Meanwhile, we hold each other's hand and together take one step at a time.

I tend to think of myself as being in the middle of a wrestling match. Like Jacob of old, I'm going round after round with a mysterious partner who won't tell me his name. (I'll be saying more about Jacob this week, but for today you can check out the story in Genesis 32.) Who is it that has me on the mat?

- Am I wrestling with Satan? Is this an attack from the enemy? "I was given a thorn in my flesh, a messenger of Satan, to torment me" (2 Corinthians 12:7).

- Or perhaps this is all just part of living in a fallen world that is marked by disease and hardship? "In this world you will have trouble" (John 16:33). "Man is born to trouble as surely as sparks fly upward" (Job 5:7).

- Or is my wrestling partner God Himself? "Is it not from the mouth of the Most High that both calamities and good things come?" (Lamentations 3:38).

- Or, is it possible that it is some cosmic interplay between all three? "The LORD said to Satan, 'Very well, then, he is in your hands; but you must spare his life.' So Satan went out from the presence of the Lord and afflicted Job with painful sores" (Job 2:6–7).

Tonight I have no answer for my own questions. But, like Jacob, I wrestle on—believing there is value and reason for the fight itself. We aren't guaranteed answers for all our questions. We are guaranteed His presence.

So, to all of you who wrestle in the dark: Jacob, Joanna, I and many others join you. You may be as confused as I am, but you are not alone.

More to come on Jacob's wrestling match in a few days.

Your fellow grappler,
John

March 18
PERMISSION GRANTED: JACOB–PART 2 (GENESIS 32)

We started with two vastly different beliefs
That launched us on a completely different trajectory.
No wonder we have a hard time connecting.

Stay with me on this. The implications are profound.

In my doctoral program last year, Professor Len Sweet reminded us that the word "Islam" means "surrender" or "submit." In contrast, the word "Israel" comes from the word "struggle."

You remember the story, right? After two decades of separation, Jacob is returning home with his family and livestock. On the final leg of the journey, he gets into a mysterious midnight wrestling match. By daybreak, Jacob is walking with a limp but believing that he has just wrestled with God Himself. Most importantly, Jacob (whose name meant "one who grasps" or "deceiver") receives a new name—Israel—"one who struggles with God." The new name obviously stuck since 4,000 years later his nation still carries the name.

Question: What kind of God is willing to be wrestled? What kind of God is willing to get on the mat with us and have it out? What kind of God would be so willing to be grappled with that He would name His people accordingly?

As Christians, our spiritual lineage winds its way back to that mystical wrestling match and the name that resulted—"one who struggles with God." We are a people who have been given the privilege—dare I say it, even the identity, as people who grapple with the Almighty. Our faith is not a blind submission to some distant sovereign power. Our faith arises out of the freedom—even the necessity—of asking hard questions, wrestling with real issues, facing life honestly and openly. This kind of faith arises in the context of relationship.

One of the powerful realities of the Christian faith is that we are invited to have a significant and genuine relationship with the living God. He wants to be known. He invites us to know Him. Again, our goal is not merely impersonal submission to a distant power. Our faith leads to genuine relationship.

Consider just a sampling of Scripture revealing God's heart on this matter:

"Now this is eternal life: that they know you, the only true God, and Jesus Christ, whom you have sent" (John 17:3).

"I want to know Christ—yes, to know the power of his resurrection and participation in his sufferings" (Philippians 3:10).

This isn't just a New Testament concept. God makes it very clear to the prophet Jeremiah,

> Let not the wise boast of their wisdom
> or the strong boast of their strength
> or the rich boast of their riches,
> but let the one who boasts boast about this:
> that they have the understanding to know me,
> that I am the LORD,
> who exercises kindness, justice
> and righteousness on earth,
> for in these I delight.
>
> Jeremiah 9:23–24

And the prophet Hosea appeals to us: "Oh, that we might know the LORD! Let us press on to know him!" (Hosea 6:3 NLT).

This is a core difference between Islam and Christianity. One does not need a relationship to submit to the authority of another; one merely accepts what comes and does what he's told. However, to have the freedom to question, challenge, cry, appeal, wonder and grapple implies and assumes that there is something significant happening relationally.

Earlier I asked: What kind of God is willing to be wrestled? The answer: A God of relationship, a God who knows us intimately and wants us to know Him intimately as well. What a privilege!

Permission granted: It is okay to ask God the hard questions and to question the answers.

"So let us come boldly to the throne of our gracious God. There we will receive his mercy, and we will find grace to help us when we need it" (Hebrews 4:16 NLT).

THE MATCH CONTINUES: JACOB–PART 3

In the Genesis 32 passage we've been considering in recent days, Jacob is making a run for a new life. He's leaving behind a twenty-year stint of working for his shrewd father-in-law and is heading home to start over. This adventure seems to create within him a new level of dependence on God.

As he journeys, he has one major cloud before him. When he left home two decades earlier, he was fleeing a murder threat from his brother, Esau. Jacob was running for his life. Now he's returning to the brother he hasn't seen since. He has to be apprehensive about what kind of reception he will receive.

As he nears his home territory, he feels it wise to send messengers ahead to notify Esau of his return. The messengers return with the ominous report that Esau is coming to meet him—with what appears to be a small army of 400 men. In no way does this sound good. Scripture tells us Jacob's response to this news: "In great fear and distress" Jacob began to take precautions (Genesis 32:7). A new start in life and a new start with God appear to be threatened by a pending attack.

This is the night that Jacob has his mystical wrestling match.

I've never studied Hebrew (the original language of most of the Old Testament), but those who have inform me that a significant play on words occurs in this part of the story. Jacob intended to spend the night sleeping alone on the bank of a stream called "Jabbok," which flows into the

Jordan River. The Jordan served as the boundary to the land of promise. In the original language, these words are eye-catching. Before Jacob (*yaaqob*) could cross the Jabbok (*yaboq*) to the land of promise, he had to wrestle (*yeabeq*). I suppose an English comparison would be the sentence, "Russell had to wrestle before crossing the Rustling River."

Maybe this is all just a bit of Bible trivia. Maybe this is merely the meandering thoughts of a sick man who has too much time on his hands. Or, perhaps just maybe, there is a spiritual truth here that some of us will find liberating. Perhaps we could conclude that on the journey to a new life, a wrestling match may be essential. Before the new comes, something of the old must die. Before we reach the Jordan we may have to be wounded at the Jabbok. Before we are given a new name, we have to first admit our old one. Before we enter the land of promise, God Himself might land us on a mat.

Leaving Jacob for a moment, I so much appreciated the honesty of the anonymous blog comment that compared two sons—one who willingly accepted life with a simple trust as it came and one who questioned and wrestled with everything. There are certainly times to be that first son—"'Tis so sweet to trust in Jesus, just to take Him at His word" we appropriately sing. But, back to Jacob, let's not miss the obvious—God picked this fight. God started it.

When we open ourselves to the possibility of wrestling with God, trite Christian answers give way to deeper life questions—we become more honest. When we become more honest, we have better conversations with God. As our conversations deepen, so does our faith. Faith born out of trite answers is shallow-rooted. Faith that is born during midnight (or midday!) wrestling matches grows roots reaching down for deeper sources of nourishment.

Lord willing, I'll soon share a personal story of what a recent wrestling match looked like in my life.

March 24
BEATING ON HIS CHEST:
JACOB–PART 4

I'm guessing that some of you are beginning to think, "Come on, Stumbo, let's get on to a new theme. We've been on this wrestling mat for a couple weeks now!" True—and I eventually will move on to other subjects—but for today I feel prompted to give a personal look at one of my recent times on the mat with God.

One of the greatest joys of my life the last twenty-three years has been being a dad. When our precious daughter, Anna, entered our lives, I would never be the same. I absolutely love our three children and consider it a huge privilege and pleasure to be their father. I am unashamedly biased that they are incredible young adults. Thus, one of the things that I enjoy most is spending time with them—even if it is limited by distance and confined to telephone calls.

Josiah, my son away at college, called last week. It was so good to hear his voice. However, after only a few minutes we gave up on the call. My voice—raspy, weak and slurred—was unintelligible to him over the phone transmission. "I'm sorry, Dad," he repeatedly had to admit, "I didn't catch that." Rather than prolong the frustration, we expressed our love and hung up.

And I was angry—not at him, but at God. I repeatedly slammed the phone on the book on my lap (which happened to be the Bible at that moment) and shouted, "I feel robbed. Robbed. ROBBED. I can't even have a decent telephone conversation with my kids." I went on to list other times and experiences I felt cheated out of. For example, I feel like I'm missing so much of my son Drew's senior year of high school. It's his last year at home, and instead of being in the weight room or on a running trail with him, I'm stuck in a chair. I feel ripped off—by God Himself—from some of the most enjoyable and meaningful moments of life.

The anger gave way to tears. "I don't want to be angry at God. How can I live angry at Him? Where else do I have to turn?"

I wish I could tell you that at that moment God showed up with an overwhelming sense of His nearness or gave a powerful insight packed with spiritual significance. Instead, heaven seemed silent.

I could relate to David who sang, "How long, Lord? Will you forget me forever? How long will you hide your face from me? How long must I wrestle with my thoughts and day after day have sorrow in my heart?" (Psalm 13:1–2).

I could feel with Isaiah who prayed, "Truly you are a God who has been hiding himself, the God and Savior of Israel" (45:15). (Remember "Israel" means "he struggles with God.") What does one do when all he hears is the hush of heaven?

If you study the passages I've quoted, David concludes his brief song with a declaration of faith, "But I trust in your unfailing love; my heart rejoices in your salvation. I will sing the Lord's praise, for he has been good to me" (Psalm 13:5–6). The circumstances hadn't changed, but David was hanging on to faith.

And to the confused Isaiah, God responds, "I have not said to Jacob's descendants, 'Seek me in vain'" (45:19). He is a God who eventually reveals Himself, even to descendants of Jacob (there is our friend again—Jacob, "the Deceiver").

In time, I have found solace in two thoughts. First, I'm grateful for the simple insight that the man in the Bible who recorded the most questions and struggles with God—the song-writing David—was also called by God "a man after my own heart" (Acts 13:22). Evidently, as David asked his penetrating "how long" kinds of questions, he was on a headlong dive into the heart of God. Deep spirituality and deep questions are not necessarily in conflict.

Second, Joanna shared a brief portion of a recent devotional with me. In a simple sentence, the author Susan Lenzkes creates a beautiful picture: "We beat on His chest from within the circle of His arms."

I pound, but I'm embraced.

From the mat,

Your friend,
John

March 27
ONE STEP TOO FAR:
JACOB–PART 5

"In all this, Job did not sin by charging God with wrongdoing" (Job 1:22).

In recent weeks I have been writing about our privilege of wrestling with God. He invites us into genuine relationship that is more than just mere submission to a sovereign power. We have access to a life-giving intimacy with our Creator. This relationship should and can be one of forthright honesty. We cannot hide anything from Him anyway (Hebrews 4:13), so transparency with our Father is our responsibility and privilege.

But, like a hiker edging his way out to the brink of a cliff to get the best view, it is possible to take one step too far on this path I've been leading us on. If I am to be a good Sherpa up this mountainside, I must issue this warning: Danger lies on this path.

As fickle humans, we can easily slip from questioning to accusation. Our honest wrestling can turn to bitter attacking. Our rightful confusion about His ways can erode to inappropriate conclusions about His character. This is where the line is crossed.

Scripture tells us that if we are to come to God we have to believe at least two core things about Him:

1. that He exists and
2. that it is His character to reward those who diligently seek Him.
   (See Hebrews 11:6.)

He is real and He is good. But when we live as if He doesn't exist or become convinced that He can't be trusted, we are just a speck of dust on a little ball in space shaking our teeny fist at the universe . . . and our Creator isn't impressed.

The people in Malachi's day "wearied" God with their words, as they doubted His goodness and justice (see Malachi 2:17; 3:13–15). Isaiah warned his audience: "Woe to those who quarrel with their Maker. . . . Does the clay say to the potter, 'What are you making?'" (45:9).

Contrast this attitude to that of the wrestling Jacob. He and his mysterious opponent have grappled through the night. As day begins to dawn, Jacob continues to cling to his challenger and says, "I will not let you go unless you bless me" (Genesis 32:26). This is the tenacity of a wrestler who believes that God exists and is a rewarder: I'm not giving in until I get a blessing!

One of our blog commenters was ahead of me. She writes about two types of struggling with God: "The first type of struggling says to God, 'I am going to persevere in this life of faith until I learn every last lesson God wants me to learn.' This is a clinging 'to' in spite of the circumstances of life. The second type of struggling is a virtual shaking of the fist in the face of God. This second type of struggling is never condoned in God's Word." Well said.

Early on in this journey, I felt that Job 1:22 was a direct word to me: "In all this, Job did not sin by charging God with wrongdoing." Only He knows—although I don't believe I have—if I've crossed this line at any low point in my journey. I want to honor God and declare His goodness, even when I don't understand Him. My heart's desire is to, like Jacob, cling to Him in this battle and to walk away with a blessing—even if I'm limping.

More on the "limp" later. Until then, show some caution on the trail.

March 31
A STRANGE GAIT: JACOB-CONCLUSION

Daybreak comes. The wrestling match is over. Jacob arises to face his brother with two things he didn't have before the wrestling match began: a new name and a limp. I believe that the new name gives him a new sense of identity—a new confidence. And the limp—well, from personal experience I can tell you that a limp is humbling and slows one down.

This duo creates a unique combination—another oxymoron. I call Jacob's new condition a "bold humility" or a "confident brokenness." I believe this is to be the strange gait of a Christ-follower. We are more than conquerors, the New Testament tells us (Romans 8:37); yet without Christ we can do nothing (John 15:5). This is a walk unique to one who walks with Christ.

When our daughter, Anna, was in high school, her success as a cross-country runner earned her an invitation to compete at a major race sponsored by Nike at their World Headquarters in Portland, Oregon. During the two-day event, each participant received a free "gait analysis" provided by Nike staff in one of their labs. I was fascinated as I watched her stride scrutinized. Little did I know what a science running and running shoes had become!

A video camera connected to a computer captured Anna's stride as she ran an eight-mile-per-hour pace on a treadmill. The recorded footage was then replayed on a large monitor in a motion slower than I knew possible. We viewed a single stride for a full thirty seconds. Each movement of the foot and ankle was noted, advice was given and a style of shoe designed specifically for her type of stride was recommended.

Perhaps we should do a little gait analysis of our own. There is no place for the Christ-follower to be a slump-shouldered, head down, "woe-is-me," false-humility foot shuffler. At the same time, an arrogant swagger is equally inappropriate. Ours is to be a stride of confidence (for greater is He that is in us than He that is in the world—1 John 4:4), yet humility (for while we were still sinners Christ died for us—Romans 5:8).

Daybreak hasn't yet arrived for me. The match appears far from over. But while I'm on the mat I want to get absolutely everything out of this that God has for me. May His refining work be complete. And someday, I want to arise from the mat with the walk of confident brokenness—a bold humility—knowing who I am in Christ yet how frail I am without Him. I may limp, but my shoulders won't be slumped.

And, by the way, I just noticed one more thing: Jacob does not receive an answer to the only question he asks (see Genesis 32:29). Maybe answers are overrated. He walks away with a blessing, but not an answer. Interesting.

Perhaps the fact that we don't receive all the answers to our deepest questions is one of the good tools God uses to keep us "limping." Yet, knowing the One who knows everything gives us the confidence to walk boldly . . . a strange gait indeed.

Walking with you,
John

April 2
TRAVELING COMPANIONS

Everywhere I go these days, I pack a few partners with me. Most notice-able is my walker or wheelchair. My right leg is fairly strong and depend-able, but there is profound muscle atrophy and some nerve damage in my left leg. As a result, a few of the primary muscles in my thigh are not oper-able—leaving my left leg weak, undependable and limited in motion. When I'm inside the house, I shuffle around with the walker. When Joanna takes me to church or the doctor, a wheelchair is essential.

Second, draped over my walker or wheelchair is my wound vacuum. This five-pound satchel is attached to a tube that runs to my right thigh. There a sponge is taped down to provide suction that keeps my wound clean. The wound is healing—albeit slowly. It has shrunk from eleven cen-timeters long to nine—in two months.

Next are the patches. As my glands are not operating, I have to supple-ment what the body normally produces via medications—some in pill and some in patch form. Every morning Joanna and I figure out where to put the three daily patches. They irritate my skin, so we have to keep rotating them.

Then, there is the infamous feeding tube. Surgically implanted into my stomach, the twelve-inch tube with its bright blue and red caps hangs out of my shirt as a continuous reminder that my swallowing function still has not returned.

Finally, I continuously carry around a paper towel or a rag. I am com-pletely unable to swallow and, yes, this even includes my own saliva. Thus,

I have the very obnoxious routine of having to spit out my own spit every few minutes. If I don't, I feel like I'm going to drown in it.

From hour to hour, room to room and place to place—wherever I go these five companions are with me 24/7. I look forward to the day when I shed them all. And I try to remember with gratitude that I've already shed about a dozen other attachments—heart monitors, respirators, etc.

Lying in bed last night, I started wondering if there isn't a parallel to be drawn here. Every one of us has the likelihood that we have some traveling companions that give evidence of the infirmities of our soul. I started asking myself, *Am I packing around bitterness?* That's an attachment I don't want to haul around with me in life. *Any grudges?* Those are completely unprofitable travel mates.

The list goes on, and my challenge turns to you as well. What are you carting around with you from day to day and place to place? Anger can be an appropriate response, but it's not to be carried from day to day (Ephesians 4:26). Revenge is never something for us to shoulder (Romans 12:17–21). Toting around a judgmental spirit not only weighs you down but others as well.

My nighttime conclusion was that envy and self-pity are probably my two most unhelpful travel mates. They keep showing up on the trail like characters from *Pilgrim's Progress*—intercepting my journey with their seductive speeches. Most days I can handle it, but every once in a while when someone talks about going out to eat, or a smell wafts from the kitchen, or the refrigerator door is opened for the seventeenth time, I about lose it with envy. It's not just the act of eating and the pleasure of taste that I miss; it is the huge social aspect of eating together that I've been cut off from for these months, leaving me feeling isolated. Envy is easily followed by self-pity—poor me. They're both unhealthy, unhelpful and unnecessary companions. Care to join me in leaving these kinds of partners in the dust?

I look forward to the day when my traveling companions once again include running shoes, a water bottle or a backpack. Meanwhile, the Spirit has better travel mates for our soul—the likes of joy, peace, kindness, gentleness and self-control (Galatians 5). May we choose our travel partners well.

On the trail with you,
John

NOTHING MORE COSTLY

April 5

During one of the sleepless portions of my night last night, a memory came into my thinking that feels appropriate to share with you as we enter Holy Week.

"So what's the deal about the blood?!" The sharp-looking, middle-aged restaurant owner stood before me with intensity in his voice.

I had just finished preaching the three morning services. Normally I stay at the front of the auditorium after I preach, but on this particular day I made my way to an exit door to greet as many people as possible. He and a friend were in church for the first time. It had been a communion morning and we had sung of the blood of Christ. From his unchurched background this was all a very new experience and his question was very appropriate.

"What's the deal about the blood?" I repeated. "You mean, Christ's blood?"

"Yeah." His eyes were locked onto me with deep interest.

It was one of those moments when I knew I needed the Spirit of God to give me an answer better than I had in my own head. In His kindness, the Spirit provided what I needed for the moment.

"Sin is a really big deal to God because it separates us from Him. It is such a big deal that the highest price had to be paid for our sin. What price is greater than blood?

And whose blood is greater than that of Christ? That's the deal about the blood. It's God's provision for us to have a relationship with Him."

He was appreciative of the answer, and after a few more sentences of cordial introduction to each other, he and his friend were on their way.

During this Holy Week, may we find a place in our hearts to truly be grateful that our God made a way possible for us to be in relationship with Him. Holiness itself stretched across the chasm created by our sin. He generously provided for us a way to be forgiven and to live in His holy presence. "For you know that it was not with perishable things such as silver or gold that you were redeemed from the empty way of life handed down to you from your ancestors, but with the precious blood of Christ, a lamb without blemish or defect" (1 Peter 1:18–19).

During this Holy Week, I encourage each of us to take some time to reflect on the kindness of such an initiating, way-making God. What would my life be like today without Him? What do I need to say or do this week to show Him my gratitude? Is there anything I need to confess—any sin I'm holding onto? "Or do you show contempt for the riches of his kindness, forbearance and patience, not realizing that God's kindness is intended to lead you to repentance?" (Romans 2:4).

And, *during this Holy Week,* if anyone reading this blog does not yet have a genuine, life-giving relationship with God through Christ, I appeal to you to come to Him today. His arms are outstretched for you. It's your move. "But God demonstrates his own love for us in this: While we were still sinners, Christ died for us" (Romans 5:8).

I don't mean to be melodramatic, but I do think I owe you the rest of the story. My question-asking acquaintance was dead before the week was over. I was stunned when I heard the news. I never knew whether he came to know the cleansing blood or not. None of us are guaranteed tomorrow. Let's be wise and do what we need to do today.

Under the blood,
John

P.S. On a personal note, this will likely be my last post for a few days, as *during this Holy Week,* I will be spending three days, six hours a day, receiving a special outpatient treatment. My doctors are not pleased with my progress; neither am I. They have decided to try a treatment that they have repeatedly referred to as "very expensive." They are hopeful that this might turn a corner for me. Interestingly, the treatment I'm receiving is the best of multiple people's blood. Expensive. Life-giving. Blood. Holy Week. Hmmm.

April 11
FORGOTTEN SATURDAY

"Joseph . . . wrapped [the body] in linen cloth
and placed it in a tomb cut in the rock. . . .
It was Preparation Day, and the Sabbath was about to begin."

Luke 23:50–54

Last night, while reflecting in bed, I began to ponder what was happening on the day *after* the Friday we call Good. This is how I understand the storyline of that odd day:

While the body of our Lord Christ lay in a tomb, the religious leaders scramble to protect themselves. In spite of it being a Sabbath, they call a meeting with Pilate to request that the tomb be guarded (Matthew 27:62–66). No doubt they also hurried to find a way to close off the suddenly exposed Holy of Holies in the temple (Matthew 27:51). This Saturday was a day to cover their own tracks and look out for their own interests.

While the body of our Lord Christ lay in a tomb, the remaining disciples of Jesus spend the Sabbath in disillusioned grief. How could everything have gone so wrong so quickly? Wasn't it just a week ago that they had received the ticker-tape parade into Jerusalem? In honor of the Sabbath, they don't walk to the grave. This Saturday was a day to be numb with grief.

While the body of our Lord Christ lay in a tomb, the crowds no doubt spend endless hours debating the events of the last few days. The guilt or innocence of Jesus was argued—and that of their religious leaders. Whatever side was taken, there was no changing things. The miracle-worker was dead.

While the body of our Lord Christ lay in a tomb, the Lord Himself is busy. In one of the most mysterious passages of the New Testament, Peter tells us, "For Christ also suffered once for sins, the righteous for the unrighteous, to bring you to God. He was put to death in the body but made alive in the Spirit. After being made alive, he went and made proclamation to the imprisoned spirits—to those who were disobedient long ago when God waited patiently in the days of Noah while the ark was being built" (1 Peter 3:18–20).

I believe this to have happened while Christ's body lay in the tomb. His body was a corpse, but His spirit was free to roam.

This is the challenge I face right now. This is the challenge many of us face. Physically, emotionally, or in some other way, we have been buried. Some key aspect of our existence feels entombed by sickness, pain, rejection, abuse, despair. The burial cloth is placed over us. We acquiesce to its suffocating presence. The stone is rolled in front of the door, and there we lie . . . defeated.

Yet, something within us beckons us to rise. Our whole existence does not need to be contained in the burial cloth. There is something deeper within us. We are not just a broken body or a broken marriage or a broken whatever. Yes, the sickness, the pain—the tomb—is real, but it's not the whole story.

Forgotten Saturday testifies to us that while His body is wrapped, motionless and medically dead, His spirit is very alive and refuses to stay behind the rock.

Again, this is my current challenge. My health has declined this last month. The treatments went well this week, but the medical staff says it will take a couple weeks before I will experience any benefit.

Meanwhile, frankly, I feel cruddy. I'm experiencing physical pain and limited strength (I haven't been up to doing physical therapy). I live with an almost overwhelming sense that everything I do is laborious. Just to shower and shave, even with Jo's kind assistance, requires far more from me than running ten miles did six months ago.

Often I've sat in my chair for two or three hours, wanting to get up and do something but unable to find the will and energy to do so. I grow weary of spitting out my saliva—some 200 times a day and then throughout the night. And I know that some of you face difficulties far worse than mine.

I can't change my physical situation. Some of you are in situations you can't change either. The call I'm issuing to myself and all of us today is to believe that our spirits can rise above our circumstance. I'm calling us to slip out from under the burial cloths, sneak out of our tombs and explore places yet unknown.

Resurrection Day is coming. I know it is. The burial cloth will not always cover us. The stone will be rolled away. We will rise—pain-free, disease-free, burden-free. But until then, Jesus still knows His way out of the tomb. May our spirits follow His lead.

April 13
ATTEMPTS AT PRACTICING
WHAT I PREACH

In my last blog, "Forgotten Saturday," I held out a challenge to all of us who are in a trial. I wrote, "The call I'm issuing to myself and all of us today is to believe that our spirits can rise above our circumstance. I'm calling us to slip out from under the burial cloths, sneak out of our tombs and explore places yet unknown."

With the way I felt this weekend, it would have been the easiest thing to just stay home and explore all the reasons to feel sorry for myself—to pull that burial cloth up tight and hang out in the grave for a while. However, the path of wisdom and integrity and healing beckoned me to join my family and get out. Let me tell you how it went—in hopes that it doesn't sound too "poor me" and leads to a word of hope.

Good Friday service was always a highlight for me as a pastor. I always loved leading congregations in this rich remembrance. I would participate again this year, but as a member of the congregation. It was difficult to watch the team assemble on the platform as I sat in my wheelchair in the very back row. The music, however, was absolutely fabulous and my spirit was drawn into worship.

Then came the moment of sharing together in communion. I asked Joanna to wheel me to the front, received the piece of bread and dipped it in the juice . . . fully knowing I had no ability to consume it. Returning to the back row, I touched the bread to my tongue, prayed a prayer and wrapped the bread in one of my rags. The morsel, now petrified, sits in my desk drawer as an odd symbol of my need and His provision. And, I wonder over Christ's words, "I will not drink again of the fruit of the vine until the kingdom of God comes" (Luke 22:18).

On Saturday evening we attended the Easter Service. Again, the difficulty of not being able to participate from the platform was overcome by the beauty and truth of the music. A month ago I reported that I had a six-note range—cracked and weak—but notes nevertheless. Sadly, I must report that by Easter I had lost all six. Here it was, the grandest celebration of the Christian year, and I had no voice to sing. My joyful noise was reduced to a whisper and a mere mouthing of the words. So, much to the consternation of the three-year-old in the pew in front of me who would not stop watching me the entire hour, I whispered and mouthed my way through the service. And I knew I would rather have a reason to sing but no voice; than have a voice and no real reason for song.

I was dreading Easter Sunday itself. It would be such a stark contrast to every other Easter our family had enjoyed, I didn't want to even think about it. But, days arrive whether we are ready for them or not. I purposely slept in and then "took" my wife and son to a family favorite, Red Lobster. Sitting at a restaurant while others are eating isn't my favorite thing to do, but I really wanted the family to have a good Easter and I was determined to not let the "burial cloths" cling too tightly. We were just concluding the pleasant meal when—bam—I got hit with a double-barrel-full-gusher bloody nose. I stuffed napkins up my nose and I asked Joanna to rush me to the van before I made a bigger scene. I was very embarrassed as we shuffled out. I defiled the sidewalk with globs of bloody spit (which my dear wife dealt with later). Forty-five minutes later we were home with the situation fully under control again; but the ordeal felt like one more blow—I can't take communion, can't sing and can't even take my family out for a decent meal without something happening.

My only solace is that I'm glad that I took every opportunity to seize the day. The setbacks definitely colored the events, but as good shadowing does on a portrait.

I finished the weekend by re-reading a chapter from Samuel Rutherford. Pastor Rutherford was exiled from his congregation in England by the state church. They sent him to a different part of the country and banned him from preaching. In his state of exile, he wrote numerous letters to friends that have been preserved in a book simply titled *Letters of Samuel Rutherford*. A few months into exile, he wrote of his inability to preach. This is what he is referring to as he speaks of his "sad silence."

He reflects, "I have wrestled long with this sad silence. I said, what aileth Christ at my service? And my soul has been at pleading with Christ. . . . But I will yield to him, providing my suffering may preach more than my tongue did. . . . In a word, I am a fool, and he is God. I will hold my peace hereafter." Samuel Rutherford, November 22, 1636

I will whisper and shuffle my way out of the public eye as long as I need to, knowing I am a fool and he is God. I will trust that my suffering may preach more than my tongue did. I will look forward to the day when my tongue can declare His praise again. And, as I have said before and will say again: I don't like the situation I am in, but He is God and He is good. Let's keep trusting Him together.

LIFE IN THE SLOW LANE

April 17

I had never heard of an ultramarathon until about five years ago when I met an Alliance pastor in California. He was a middle-aged non-runner who decided to jog to his mailbox one day. The next day he jogged a little farther. Then a mile. Eventually he was running 50Ks (31 miles) and 50-milers. I thought he was crazy, but he planted a seed that took root in my head, and two years later I was running some of the same races he was. He's the one who taught me the classic ultramarathon runner's motto: "Start out slowly and taper off from there." One key to successful long-distance running is to know your pace. Go out too hard and fast and you'll pay for it severely on some long, lonely miles of the trail.

A year ago this weekend, I ran a 60K race in Sisters, Oregon. The Peterson Ridge Rumble starts at the high school and heads down a lonely road before taking a sharp right turn up into the hills. A couple-thousand-foot climb awaits the runner. On this particular day, the trail on the upper level was covered with ice and snow—making for interesting running on some stretches. It also made for a great resource for keeping cool. As the temperature climbed to 70 degrees (hot for an ultramarathon in April), I repeatedly filled my hat with snow and ran with its cooling drips running down my body. The snow felt marvelous and kept my body from overheating. In the end, it wasn't my strongest race, but I finished it and went on last summer to rank in the top ten of ultramarathon runners in my age division in the state of Oregon.

Fast forward a year. I am at the clinic for yet another blood draw. As our routine goes, Joanna pulls the van up to the clinic's main entrance, sets up my walker, helps me out of the passenger seat and drives away to find a parking space. My job is to get inside the clinic and wait for her in an awaiting wheelchair. As I make my way toward the double entrance doors, I sense movement to my right. A woman with a walker (the nifty kind with four wheels and a seat) blows past me like I was standing still. She looks to be 85 years old and 85 pounds. I am left eating her dust. As she passes me she turns and spits on my shoe (okay, I made that part up). Seriously, as she passed, I thought, "I knew I was slow, but this is ridiculous."

Joanna soon joined me in the clinic; I got my blood drawn and hobbled my way back to the entrance while she retrieved the van. Meanwhile I was still thinking about Ms. 85/85—*Blown away by granny. Wow, I must really be slow.* I have reason to be cautious. Significant muscles, including those in my left leg, are still nonfunctioning, leaving my knee vulnerable to buckling at any moment. I've fallen a few times as a result. Therefore, I move cautiously. Besides that, I'm just plain weak a lot of days and don't have the strength to move with much speed or agility.

Ultramarathons and clinic visits with my walker lead me to lessons on healing. They remind me that in the recovery process you have to accept your own pace. In time you may be able to quicken your pace, but for today it is what it is—accept it.

Healing is not a speed sport. The luge, NASCAR, the 4 x 400 relay— those are speed sports, but not healing. For all of us who are in a crisis— be it emotional, physical, financial, relational or whatever—our instinct is to get over it and out of it as fast as possible. We just want to feel better— now! And, too often we will compromise or cheat ourselves in attempts to speed up the process. It doesn't work.

Healing comes delivered in a package called "time," which often appears to have way too much tape on it. We seize the package and start grabbing all the sharp instruments we can find—moving from butter knife, to scissors, to the hunting knife—to get into those contents as quickly as possible. I think I've even heard a few chain saws ripping away occasionally. The problem of course is that if we use a too aggressive instrument, we'll damage the goods inside before we ever reach them. Healing and speed rarely go together.

One exception: If God chooses to touch the heart or body supernaturally, healing can happen in an instant. Joanna and I have a little phrase we will say to each other when we are discouraged—"one touch." By that we mean it doesn't look like our situation will ever end some days, but all it would take is one touch from Christ and I would be completely whole. He may or may not choose to give it, but I am at every moment just one touch away from complete deliverance. So are you. We'll trust Him to do what is right and what brings Him the most glory.

Back to my theme: During my years of long-distance running, I injured myself a number of times because, in my impatient zeal, I didn't allow enough recovery time after a long race or major workout. I ignored the fundamental lesson that our bodies don't grow stronger by exercise alone—if they did, we'd grow stronger and stronger every mile we ran. No, our muscles grow stronger through a vital combination of exercise and rest. It is in the recovery time that the muscles rebuild. Hurry this process to your own demise. I speak from experience.

Healing takes time. We all have our own pace. For most of us that pace should be a slow one. Accept it. Ignore the voices that say to you, "You should be over that by now." And resist your own temptation to make it a speed event.

At the same time, read yourself well. Make sure you aren't stuck. Wallowing in the mire of our pain is not the answer. Pick up that walker and slide it forward another eighteen inches, even if granny is leaving tread marks on your tennis shoes. Pack a little snow in your hat if you need to. Resist the temptation to use it to fire a snowball at geriatric sprinters. Find your pace, keep your stride and know that you are moving toward a healthier future.

"Start out slowly and taper off from there" may be the advice you need for the trail you're on today.

THE BEAUTY OF A FULFILLED VOW

April 21

(Warning: The preacher got long-winded today.)

A businessman wandered into a doughnut shop in Grand Saline, Texas, one morning and ended up with far more than a doughnut. He noticed a young farm couple was seated at a table. The man was wearing overalls and she wore a gingham dress. After finishing their doughnuts, he got up to pay the bill, and the businessman noticed she didn't get up to follow him.

After paying, the man came back and stood in front of her. She put her arms around his neck, and he lifted her up, revealing that she was wearing a full-body brace. He lifted her out of her chair and backed out the front door to the pickup truck, with her hanging from his neck. As he gently put her into the truck, everyone in the shop watched. No one said anything until an employee remarked in almost a holy whisper, "He took his vows seriously."

I've thought of that story often as I look into my wife's eyes. There she is kneeling on the floor again for the thousandth time putting on my socks or caring for my dry skin. I know, I know, she has been very clear that she would rather be a nurse than a widow and is grateful to have me around. I know, I've heard her say it repeatedly that she is happy to serve me and senses that she is serving Christ in the process. All true. All healthy. All beautiful.

But when another day is done—another day of having her assist me from showering to dressing, to getting down the stairs, through three or four feedings, through countless medications, to picking up what I've dropped on the floor and can't reach for myself, to assisting in my therapy, to delivering me to yet another doctor's visit . . . and on the list goes. When another day is done and my head hits the pillow, I know one thing: She took her vows seriously.

"For better or for worse, in sickness and in health," we stated. We were so young—what did we know? She was still a teenager. Having graduated from high school at 16, she was halfway through college by the time most girls were still figuring out what to wear to prom. I was accused by my buddies of robbing the cradle, but I knew a good thing when I saw it. After two years of courtship, we stood before 400 friends and family members and youthfully declared our intentions for the rest of our lives.

Ridiculous, actually.

We didn't have enough wisdom, experience, foresight or maturity to make such a declaration. Perhaps that is why God allows a little love blindness to capture young couples. If we really knew what we were saying at the moment, we'd be shaking in fear, looking for the lawyer's fine print or excusing ourselves to go find a bathroom. "For better or for worse, for richer or for poorer, in sickness and in health, 'til death do us part." Wow. Bold words for kids barely old enough to get a rental car.

Yet, twenty-six years later, I gratefully declare that she is living out those vows and I consider myself blessed. I knew I was marrying a woman of character on that snowy Minnesota December day in 1982, but I had no idea just how much I would benefit from that character.

So celebrate with me today a woman who has chosen a lifestyle that doesn't revolve around herself, has chosen to serve a husband whose needs are unrelenting, took her vows seriously and has done so without complaint. And who, by the way, is very uncomfortable with this kind of acknowledgement. (Too bad, Honey; it's my blog!)

Allow me to go a few paragraphs further. Allow me to put my pastoral hat back on and preach a bit. I see this as an opportunity to offer a few challenges. Some of these things may seem so obvious that I don't need to put them in print. On the other hand, I'm not sure where these kinds of messages are being clearly spoken these days, so here goes:

First, I appeal to all singles in pursuit of a marriage relationship: Look for Christ-like character above all else. Compatibility is good, but you might find yourself compatible—enjoying similar hobbies, conversing easily—with someone who has no character depth. Wealth is nice, but don't chase it in marriage. To be courted is exciting, but without character you'll eventually end up in another court. Attractiveness is a bonus; hopefully you see some physical beauty in the other person. I certainly did and do with Joanna. But can I remind us that we don't marry just a face—we marry a complex person. Beauty fades. Character blossoms. Marry character.

Second, I appeal to married couples who are struggling right now. I know that there are, at times, legitimate reasons to call it quits. However, this list is much smaller than society is telling us. "I just don't love him like I once did" isn't on the legitimate list. "She's not the same person I married" isn't either. Of course she's not the same person she was. She's been married to *you* for twenty years. That's bound to change a person! And, if she hasn't changed for the better, maybe *you* had something to do with it—not everything, but something.

"We've drifted apart." Well, grab an oar and start paddling back. Don't believe the lie that you will automatically be happier alone. Don't believe the lie that you'll certainly be happier with that other person across the office. Don't believe the lie that happiness is the ultimate goal.

I need to give another word to married couples: Some of us have easier marriage relationships than others. Joanna and I have never had an easy marriage. We've had to work at it from the very beginning. Countless times we've had to come back together and say, "Okay, let's talk this through. Where did we get off track?" But that's the key: We've kept coming back. Each time we grew a little stronger as individuals and healthier as a couple. Each time was another blow to the enemy who is seeking to destroy every Christian marriage. If you have a marriage that ranks high on the compatibility scale—you naturally agree on subjects, converse easily, enjoy the same things—consider it a blessing and a loss. It is a blessing because you have an ease of life others will never experience and a loss because you are missing out on some character development opportunities—although life has a way of dishing out plenty of them, so you'll catch up to the rest of us.

Next, a word to those who have known the trauma of divorce. I don't know your story. It's not mine to know. Some of you, no doubt, did the right thing. It was an act of courage and character to remove yourself from the nightmare you were in. Others no doubt bailed out early—God had more in store but you didn't hang around long enough to experience it. And some of you had no choice in the matter as your spouse ended the relationship regardless of your efforts.

Whatever your analysis is of your situation, use it as an entrance into a pursuit of deeper character and greater intimacy with God. A door has been opened, inviting you to walk in healthy places. Take Him up on the offer. And, somehow, may God grant you the grace to not live with a label. God doesn't look upon you as "divorcee" but as "child" (for those who have come to Him for salvation) or as "lost lamb" (for those who have not yet done so). Wise are those who can see themselves as God sees them.

And, here's a word to us all: In a world glutted with contracts, lawsuits, fine print and disclaimers—often necessary, I know—let us simply be people of our word. Nothing crushes a child like a broken promise. Few things mar a Christian businessperson's reputation like unfulfilled commitments. Some of us mean well, but we're far too flippant in what we say. We have good intentions; we just don't have our act together well enough to carry them out. Isn't it time we own up or shut up? Others of us are good at keeping our commitments, until we realize it is going to be inconvenient or hurt.

Finally, back to thoughts about my wife's kindness to me: Caregivers, you rock! I celebrate you. You are giving your life so that others have a higher quality of life . . . a level we in no way could attain on our own. This is a noble thing you are doing. May God give you the same grace He has given to my wife and count it a genuine privilege to serve. You're not just serving us; you are serving Christ Himself. God bless you as you do.

April 23
POWERFUL PICTURES

Some of you have heard me tell the story of a Sunday morning prayer time in my office that was very significant for me. For years now, every Sunday before the early service a highly dedicated group of praying saints gathers to intercede for the church. They have been a great encouragement to me and a behind-the-scenes blessing to the entire church family.

During one of these prayer times a member prayed, "Lord, as John gets up to preach this morning, I see him running across the stage with a spear in his hand thrusting it into the heart of the enemy." Very cool. She had no way of knowing how significant this would be for me. You see, up to this point I had been living with a different mental image when I preached. Our church has grown to the point that we have five services in our worship center. The preacher for the weekend preaches all five. I'm not sure where it came from, but somewhere in this preaching journey I developed a picture in my head of a boxer heading in for another round in the ring. Prior to preaching the fourth service, for example, I'd often say to myself, "Two rounds to go." This, however, was a very tiring mental picture for me. Picturing myself as a boxer didn't inspire, strengthen or motivate me. Rather, it drained energy from me. It felt accurate but unhelpful.

The moment my praying friend suggested a different picture, everything changed. "Running across the platform chucking spears into the heart of Satan? Yeah! I want to do that five times! Let me up there. Let me preach!"

I quickly traded a draining mental picture for an empowering one, and it made a difference in my energy, attitude and the preaching itself.

These mental pictures I'm referring to are often called "metaphors." We use them far more often in life than we may be aware. We may not be conscious of them, but they can shape and drive much of our lives.

For example, through the practical teaching of Peacemaker Ministries, I realized that I viewed any disagreement as battle. Any quarrel that, for example, Joanna and I would have was (in my mind) a negative experience of combat. The friends from Peacemaker came along, however, and suggested that conflict is an opportunity: for the relationship to deepen, understanding to enlarge, God to be glorified, etc. What a difference this single shift in thinking makes! With the "battle" metaphor I enter the disagreement in a defensive posture, ready to win or lose, but without hope of anything good coming from it. The "opportunity" metaphor places me mentally in a position of expectancy—some good is going to come out of this and besides, she's not my enemy; she's my ally. We'll work this out.

Upon identifying that metaphors are so powerful in shaping our lives, I began to ask others about the images that shape theirs. One youth pastor admitted that he viewed himself as a crack cocaine dealer—pumping the kids up every Wednesday with a Jesus hit and then needing to do it all over again the next week. He admitted that a different metaphor could serve both him and his teens better. One woman realized that her picture of her marriage was of two people clinging to each other on the deck of a sinking ship. A pastor acknowledged that he saw his ministry as a "glorious headache" where he saw the glory of God at work in the midst of the worst of what humanity does and is.

With eyes open to metaphors, you'll also find that people in the Bible referred to them as well. In Isaiah 38, for example, Hezekiah had been deathly ill and viewed his life like a tent that had been pulled down and taken from him. Jeremiah was getting upset with the sermons God had him preach, but he couldn't stop because he felt like they were fire in his bones (Jeremiah 20). Mental pictures—metaphors—are descriptors that can motivate or immobilize us. They've been part of the human journey for a long time.

I'm sharing all of this today for two reasons. First, I want to challenge you to consider the metaphors that are shaping your life. You get to choose them. No one is making you believe them, but most of us haven't clearly identified them. Upon recognizing a metaphor in your life, ask yourself, "Is this metaphor working for me or against me? Does it empower or drain?"

If your metaphor isn't serving you well, ask God to help you form a better one. Give it some prayer time, mental reflection and/or an excuse to have a conversation with a friend over a cup of coffee.

The second reason I share this today is let you know that the Lord helped me with a metaphor shift lately. I have to admit that for the last few months, my metaphor for my illness was not a healthy one. The illness hit me so quickly and powerfully that my metaphor was that of being hit by a train or being beaten by a baseball bat. How's that for a way to start each day? Obviously, my metaphor was not empowering me to face life with energy. It also was influencing my view of God. I knew I needed something different. I prayed. God answered. It's not a new metaphor or one that is unique for me—metaphors don't have to be. It has, however, significantly reshaped my thinking.

The new metaphor? I'm not being beaten by a baseball bat. I am a piece of clay on a pottery wheel in the tender, loving hands of the Master Artisan. I rather liked the pot He had spent the first forty-eight years creating, but in His wisdom He decided to do some serious remolding. He softened the clay, cranked up the wheel and bore down to reshape this middle-aged man. I picture His hands pressing, forming, guiding, shaping—often working in silence, but always in love and wisdom. I throw up a few appeals and questions from time to time; but I'm also trying to learn to sit still—to trust Him—and let His finger press in deeply.

Isaiah prayed, "Yet you, Lord, are our Father. We are the clay, you are the potter; we are all the work of your hand" (64:8). This is my life.

Thanks for trusting the Potter with me.

May 2
ONE TWIG IN THE FAMILY TREE–
PARTS 1 AND 2

Part 1

I recently received a twenty-three-page history of our genealogical records from one of my cousins. For a list of names, it was fascinating. Now if it were a list of names of your family, I wouldn't have made it past the first page, but there seems to be a common human longing to know from whence we came. For this reason adoptive children often reach a point in life where they want to find their birth family. We realize that the "who am I" question is answered at least in some small way by the "where did I come from" question.

The document traces our family back almost 400 years to the region of Alsace, France. It appears that they were simple people, living in little villages with big names like Zutzendorf, Langensoultzbach and Gumbrechtshoffen. No royalty or dignitaries or counts are listed—just normal families baptizing their eight children at the Lutheran church in town. We have no record of the employment of many of the families, but at least two of the men were shepherds. One of the women, Anna Maria, tragically died when she froze to death on a country lane. Rural people. Simple people.

For some reason undisclosed in the document, some of these simple people started getting on ships such as *The Dragon* and *The Loyal Judith* to sail to Philadelphia to start a new life. From there they continued to venture west—Shenandoah, Virginia, then Ohio and then finally the Stumbo Mecca: Boone, Iowa.

En route through the generations, men of our clan would fight in the Revolutionary War, the War of 1812 and the Civil War (Union Army, 83rd Ohio Infantry). In fact, my great-great grandfather, James Quinn Stumbaugh (properly pronounced with a solid German guttural sound—like you are getting ready to spit) got his hat shot off in a Civil War encounter. (It does cause one to wonder: If there had been a two-inch difference in a bullet's trajectory, would I have ever come into existence? Nah, I'm not going to waste my time contemplating that one.)

It was this great-great grandfather James and his Army chaplain brother Joshua who had the audacity to change their name to "Stumbo." We don't know their rationale. Did they have to buy too many vowels on *Wheel of Fortune?* Did they get tired of clearing their throats every time they said their name? Did they not consider that "Stumbaugh" rhymes with, well nothing really, but "Stumbo" would forever be coupled with "Dumbo"? We don't know what they were thinking. But we do know that some of the rest of the clan wasn't happy and refused to speak to them anymore. Their father, with the humble name of George Washington Stumbaugh, never knew of their decision for he had died years earlier from drinking hot pepper, which he reportedly was using as a medical treatment to cure an illness. Nobody said we were smart.

The Stumbo clan: simple people, shepherds and soldiers, traveling west, stirring up a little trouble and making a few dumb decisions as they went . . . hmm, sounds like I fit in this family just fine. My twig is quite comfortable on that kind of a tree.

Part 2

Just as we have a family heritage, we have a spiritual one as well. For those of us who are Christ followers, our heritage meanders its way back to a gruesome cross outside Jerusalem.

Joanna and I were talking this week about the fact that our faith is a suffering faith—it was born out of pain. The central symbol of Christianity is a cross—a place of suffering. This is the tree upon which our twig grows.

No wonder Peter writes, "Dear friends, do not be surprised at the fiery ordeal that has come on you to test you, as though something strange were happening to you. But rejoice inasmuch as you participate in the sufferings of Christ, so that you may be overjoyed when his glory is revealed" (1 Peter 4:12–13).

More on this tomorrow.

May 3
ONE TWIG IN THE FAMILY TREE– PART 3 (CONCLUSION)

Yesterday I recounted the story of the Stumbo lineage. There are many directions I could go with thoughts like those running through my head. But for tonight, here's where my mind is taking me:

One ancestor died from freezing. One from hot pepper. One escaped death—for a season—by the height of his hat. But the records all have a sense of finality to them. They all have a little dash after their birth date and following that date is a number; be it 1714 or 1914. Life was granted. Life, on earth, came to an end.

I think that most of us accept our mortality. We may avoid thinking about it, but we don't deny it. We accept that we're not designed to live in this mortal body indefinitely. Life is given to us—it is ours to seize—but it has an end date. We can live with that.

And I think for most of us we know that at some point in the journey of life we will suffer. None of us escapes this world pain-free. We know this. We accept that we'll all eventually be dealt a card or three with the face of pain on it.

But here's the wildcard: What we hope for is as many good years as possible. We know we'll eventually have some issue that brings about our demise, but we hope (and sometimes demand) that we'll have lots of good years before that point. We hope and pray for as little pain as possible for as long as possible. We have a deep and universal drive for comfort and self-preservation. This is not a bad thing. In fact, to not have this drive is very unhealthy.

For this reason, I don't think I would have struggled nearly as greatly with my condition if it had hit my healthy body at 78 rather than 48. At 78 I think I would have more easily accepted a major blow to my health, but at 48 I feel cheated. I have so many more sermons to preach, races to run, fish to catch, meals to enjoy, etc. They were 48 good years—but, hey, only 48! I was counting on quite a few more. I had plans. I had speaking engagements lined up. I had a doctoral program to finish and a building program, too. I had assumptions that tomorrow would look a lot like to-day. I had various visions for my future, but none of them—not a single one—included hospitalization, illness or being on the disabled list.

During a day of reflection last year, I worked on a Life Plan—estab-lishing some goals, rearranging some priorities. In the entire document, I wrote nothing about "learn to suffer with grace" or "learn to endure pain and hardship." I didn't see it coming. I didn't want to see it coming. Sure, it would be mine to suffer someday, but not now—not at 48.

My twig hangs on a family tree with a rather odd name, but a tree of which I'm proud. My twig looks a little rough from being nibbled on by a "bug," but it is clinging to the Branch and seeking to bear some fruit while I still have life flowing through me. I didn't plan or desire that this fruit be born out of pain, but it often is. Every woman who has given birth to a child will tell you this.

Conclusion

I'll confess I don't know where to land this blog. Do I challenge all of you who are in good health to seize the day and enjoy every moment? It's a good point, but it's made often enough and sometimes can become burden-producing—"Am I grateful enough? Am I missing the moment?"

Do I warn that "your time is coming, so brace up"? No. That's no way to live. I'm glad I was carefree and clueless six months ago as I joyfully ran ten miles through a county park on what would be my last day of health. We don't improve the quality of our lives by living with some foreboding fear hanging over us like a thundercloud ready to burst at any moment.

Should I make some point about leaving your legacy in the family tree? Again, a good point, but one that is often made. We know we want to leave a blessing and end well.

I guess the landing point for me tonight is that I'm slowly realizing that I need to learn to live the life I've been given. This does not mean that I am resigned to be in this condition for the rest of my life. I'll still pray for healing and do my part in the healing process. But (to change the picture from family trees to a deck of cards) I have to play the cards I have been dealt. This is my family. This is my heritage. This is my illness. This is my story. This is what I have been dealt. I can be strategic in how I play my hand, but I don't get to choose it. I can pray that the Dealer will throw me a new card now and then. I'm looking for a discard pile for a few I've got right now. But day by day the game plays on and I, alone, choose how I will play it out. I don't get to play your hand, nor do you mine. We sit at the same table. We share the same deck. We trust the Dealer. We have choices to make.

Play thoughtfully, but don't over-think it. Play boldly, but risk wisely. Play together; it's legal to partner up in this game. Play for His glory—we win when the Dealer wins.

Okay. I've played my card for the night. It's your turn. I'll try to be back in a few days.

May 7
PRAYER-WORRIERS:
THOUGHT-POWERED–PART 1

Joanna will tell you that I've been known to argue with the doctors from time to time. I think I'm nice enough about it, but I do push back, question and seek for some assurance that their next plan for my life is a good one. So it was only natural that when the word "colonoscopy" came up, I balked. I wasn't going to just take this lying down; I needed assurance that such an invasion was essential. Words like "routine," "no big deal" and other attempts at calming me were unhelpful. But then it was made clear, "It appears that you are losing blood somewhere—we need to check you out." Okay. I concede. You win.

The doctors decided that since they were already probing around, they might as well run a camera down my throat too. I've had some discomfort lately in that region so I didn't object. I'm always a sucker for two-for-one deals anyway. The date was set for Tuesday, May 5.

As many of you know, the happy procedure actually begins the night before when you have the joy of drinking *three liters* of intestinal Drano. For once my inability to swallow was a blessing. Every ten minutes we dumped more flush into my tube and every hour throughout the night I was doing a flush of a different kind. A Depends wouldn't have been a bad idea—but a guy has his pride, you know.

Tuesday morning arrived and I headed into the outpatient center trudging like a criminal going to court—to face the sentence and get it over with. Posters of body parts surrounded me. This is not my favorite choice in wall décor. The medical staff was very kind and nonchalant about it all—acting as if it really were "routine" and "no big deal." What a conspiracy.

When the doctor arrived, he was very gracious—and he was wearing a *tie* as he prepared to run hoses around my body. (I'd be wearing hazmat gear if I had that job.) He went out of his way to assure me that he would use different hoses for the throat and the colon. Good plan.

Based on previous experience, I told him that I didn't need the full dose of sedatives. In the past, normal amounts have knocked me out more than they do the average person.

This proved to be a mistake. As the procedure began, I was fully aware of what he was doing and of the strange noises coming out of my mouth. "Give him more sedative," the doctor said. This was followed by more awareness. More noises. "I'm not even around the first corner yet," I heard the doctor say. "Give him more." Evidently I was still asking him questions all the way to the second procedure. Suffice it to say that by the time he was done, he had given me twice the normal dose of sedatives.

I woke up some time later in the recovery room (decorated with more body part posters) with my lovely wife at my side. She said I looked *really* relaxed.

The colonoscopy revealed that I had irritation in the intestines, likely from decreased circulation at some point—presumably from ICU days—but it looked like it was in the healing process. "Non-specific colitis," I think he called it. I believe this to be doctor-speak for "I found something but don't really know what it is." He didn't seem too concerned. Meanwhile, no tumors or blockages were found. This is good.

Down the throat he found ulcers in my esophagus—possibly from my medication. These were new. We're changing a few meds to try to alleviate this. I'll be fine.

Now in case you haven't picked up on it already, let me just come out and admit that I was worried about this whole ordeal. From the moment the word "colonoscopy" was mentioned until the sedative finally took control, I worried my way through this entire experience.

Worry is one of those vices that we know has no value, but some of us resort to it habitually. Why? There must be some reason that we would choose to go to a place that is unhelpful and unhealthy.

As I've reflected on this in recent days, I'm concluding that the reason I accept worry as a legitimate tool is because it gives me a sense of control. Of course, there is no truth in that thought—I had no control of the procedure or its findings—unless I bailed out completely. Although inaccurate, this is what worry convinces me of: If I stew over the issue, I haven't lost control. It is somehow in my grasp. Dumb, but powerful.

What are we to do with worry when it arises within us? The spiritual answer of course is found in Philippians 4:6. Paul instructs us: "Do not be anxious [worry] about anything, but in every situation . . . with thanksgiving, present your requests to God."

Some of us have discovered a remarkable ability, however, to completely destroy the effectiveness of Paul's solution by co-mingling worry with prayer. You've heard of *prayer-warriors?* Some of us are *prayer-worriers.* We finish out a time of prayer where we've verbalized our stress and become more convinced than ever that we indeed do have a major issue on our hands; then we head out into our day not really sure if we truly talked to God or only ourselves about the matter. Either way the issue still rests solidly on our shoulders.

The solution to worry is more difficult than a mere "just pray about it." We're told two verses later that we have the power to choose what we think about: "Whatever is true, whatever is noble, whatever is right, whatever is pure, whatever is lovely, whatever is admirable—if anything is excellent or praiseworthy—think about such things" (Philippians 4:8). We decide what thoughts we will allow to roam around in our heads, and we would be better off if we chose thoughts from this list. As you noticed, worry isn't on it.

Interestingly, these two verses surround the promise that the "peace of God, which transcends all understanding, will guard your hearts and your minds in Christ Jesus" (4:7). As we often find in Scripture, we have our part and God has His. There are some things only we can do (pray, choose our thoughts carefully) and there are some things only He can do (grant peace). Wise are those who differentiate between the two.

More on our thought life in a day or three. Meanwhile, anyone else out there believing the lie that worry gives control?

Working toward a healthier tomorrow—for all of us.

Your friend,
John

May 9
INEDIBLE DREAMS:
THOUGHT-POWERED–PART 2

I'm now approaching the six-month mark since the last time I ate food. I remember the moment well. The nurse brought me an Ensure/ice cream shake. I would have eaten the whole thing if I had known it was my last meal for months to come. In the early months I had strong cravings—especially for beverages. A can of Diet Coke sat for days on the hospital window ledge mocking me, calling to me, taunting me—and I don't even drink Diet Coke. Beer ads on NFL games looked so incredibly inviting—and I don't even drink beer. You get the idea. I would have dumped anything available down my throat if I could have.

Through the months, the cravings have lessened in intensity, but my mind has done a variety of things to process this unique experience. Lately, my mind has been trying to sort all of this out in the form of dreams. I don't need a Daniel to tell me what is going on in my head in the night. Here are some dreams that I've had recently:

- I am speaking at a conference. It is mealtime. I am just a few feet away from a wonderful buffet, but I can't get past the cashier because I don't have my meal ticket.

- The pizza is on the roof—warm and waiting. I scramble up the ladder to grab a few slices. My ladder was too short. I can't reach it.

- Women are making wonderful fruit salads—four different kinds. But they aren't done and it isn't time to eat so we are forbidden to touch them.

- The fruit bowl is unlike anything I had ever seen—with an apple so big people came by with knives just to take a slice. I take some grapes—wonderful grapes—but they kept falling on the floor before I can get them to my mouth.

- A potluck dinner is planned in a large auditorium. After it begins, 1,000 youths show up without food. There is nowhere near enough food for the crowd. I race to find other leaders to try to find a solution. They are nowhere to be found. I and hundreds of others were left unfed.

- An apple lies on the ground. It looks fine from a distance. I am determined to eat it. I pick it up only to find that it is thoroughly rotten. With great disappointment, I drop it back to the ground.

Okay, you get the idea. Food has become a theme of the night in my head. Last night's dream took a new twist. For some medical reason unknown to me I had to eat a crane fly. (For those not from the Pacific Northwest, a crane fly looks a lot like a mosquito—only about ten times bigger, with a wing span of a few inches for the midsize ones. Fortunately, they don't bite.) In my dream, I caught a crane fly, found two small squares of Hershey's chocolate on the counter and a strawberry in the sink. And, you guessed it, I ate. After being withheld dream food for weeks, my first dream meal was a crane fly sandwich. Nice. Maybe I need Daniel after all.

My mind isn't just working at night. I have a lot of time to think these days. Just because the body doesn't have the energy to get out of the chair doesn't mean that the mind is shut down as well. In these long days of "recovery," I'm realizing more than ever the power of the mind.

I'm not telling you anything you don't already know, but I am feeling it with a greater certainty and clarity than ever: We must be very intentional about the thoughts we allow to linger in our heads. It is self-damaging for us to just let thoughts roam unrestrained. We, alone, decide what we will think about.

This becomes even more significant when you begin to realize that not every thought we have originates with us. I believe that many of the thoughts that enter our minds come from outside sources—other people, our environment, headlines, God and even demons. Just because a thought enters our head doesn't mean that we have to allow it to stay. In fact, this is an essential aspect of emotional health and spiritual growth—choosing which thoughts get to hang around and which thoughts must be quickly rejected.

Some of you may have been surprised to read that I said demons can plant thoughts in our heads. Certainly my old sinful nature has all the evil necessary to think the worst of thoughts, so I'd caution us from blaming everything on the demonic world. However, we are in a spiritual battle, and one of the most decisive battlefronts is between our ears.

You'll remember the story of when Jesus was explaining to His disciples that He would be betrayed, crucified and resurrected. Peter took Jesus aside and began to rebuke Him: "This shall never happen to you!" (Matthew 16:22). Jesus' response is very strong: "Get behind me, Satan! You are a stumbling block to me; you do not have in mind the concerns of God, but merely human concerns" (16:23). Evidently, Peter's verbalized thoughts were of satanic origin.

So let me repeat: The way we handle our thought life is a fundamental determinant of our emotional health and spiritual growth. I do better some days than others. The last couple of days have provided extra challenge. It seems that I've been bombarded with discouraging and embittering thoughts. One by one I reject them, but I'll confess that this gets tiring. However, better to fight the battle and land in a good place than to live under the dark clouds that threaten.

More on this tomorrow. Meanwhile, happy dreams and healthy thoughts to you.

$\mathscr{May}$ 10
GETTING SPECIFIC:
THOUGHT-POWERED–PART 3

As I write, I feel like I'm walking a fine line between being real (transparent, authentic) and being too forthcoming (open, revealing). You'd expect Dave Barry to write about the details of his colon, but not your pastor. Yet I think you understand my motive: I don't want what I write to be stuck behind some fence of obscurity or irrelevance. My challenges and yours are real-body, real-experience, real-pain, real-life challenges . . . so I'll keep writing in as graphic of terms as I feel appropriate. Too often the power of the Christian faith is lost in a sea of spiritual language—it all sounds wonderful, but in the end no one has a clue what we're talking about and certainly no idea how to live it out.

I've been writing for the past week on our thought lives. We are thought-powered creatures. Our thoughts empower or dishearten us. Our thoughts release or restrict us. And, I admitted that I've felt like I've been in a brain-battle recently.

To take this from the theoretical to the tangible, let me reveal some of the specific thought challenges I've faced. Here's what's been going on in my head lately:

- "I'll never get any better. I'll never swallow again. I'll be stuck on a feeding tube for the rest of my life." That demoralizing thought has to be rejected and replaced with something better, such as,

"I don't know that. I have no idea what the future holds. I'm just one touch away from complete healing. Besides, the doctors are still working on my behalf; better days may be coming."

- "Why does he get to do that and I don't? I'd love to be doing what he's doing now; instead I'm stuck in this chair." These are the kinds of envious thoughts that plague me. Whether it is working in my yard or playing tennis or speaking at a conference, it is hard to not feel completely sidelined and left out of all the things I once loved in life. It is far easier to mourn with those who mourn than to rejoice with those who rejoice—yet, rejoice is exactly what I must choose to do as someone does something I am unable to do.

- In the night, at times, one of the most hideous of my delusions from the ICU days tries to sneak back in and overwhelm me. I'll spare you the details—suffice it to say it is suffocating in nature. I reject the thought and begin to pray or call up a song to memory.

I think that sampling is enough to give you a feel for the kinds of things I'm talking about. Your list will be completely different. Just know that not every thought you think should be allowed to hang around. Your mind can become a minefield if you let it take you wherever it will.

"Set your minds on things above," Paul tells us in Colossians 3. Our thoughts are ours to control. Our thoughts are our responsibility. Maybe it really is the "thought" that counts.

I have one more thing to say on this topic—hopefully my head and fingers will be able to bring it together in the next day or so.

May 10
THOUGHT-POWERED–
CONCLUSION

One of the roles in life that I have enjoyed the most is that of being an uncle. I absolutely love being "Uncle John." I was only seven when my sister made me an uncle for the first time. I loved that little baby and the many that followed. By the time I was old enough to have kids of my own, I was uncle to a whole clan. And, major bonus, when I got married I was suddenly "uncle" many times over again from all the nephews and nieces from Joanna's side of the family. Jackpot!

When the kids were small, I'd wrestle with them on the floor or give piggyback rides. As they grew older, we graduated to fishing boats and pizza places. Unfortunately, I've rarely lived within hundreds of miles of them, so our contacts are intermittent. But, I seize most any chance I have to be with them. They are all such cool people.

On this Mother's Day weekend, I've been thinking about two of these young adult couples to whom I am "uncle." They are fine Christians, delightful people with solid marriages and good jobs. You would like them as your neighbors. I would like them as mine! The one thing their hearts lack is the ability to have a child. For whatever reason, God has not granted their multi-year prayer for life in the womb.

I've been writing this past week on our thought lives—convinced that our spiritual, emotional and even physical health is greatly impacted by the thoughts we allow to linger within us. We must not accept every thought that comes into our heads as our own or valid. I've shared specifically some of the mental battles I've been fighting.

To take us one step further in this discussion, I must state what is obvious to some but neglected by many: **Our most important thoughts are our thoughts about God.** How we view God largely dictates how we view all of life. One person views God as stern and angry. As a result, this person may become a rigid but graceless law-keeper. Another person views God as "the old man upstairs," friendly but distant and uninvolved in our daily affairs. As a result, this person may tend to live independently, believing that our lives are under our own control. You get the point.

In this world, some things are secondary causes and some are root causes. Our view of God is a root cause. It is the launching pad for many other thoughts and beliefs. Alter your view of God and many other views will change as well.

Few things more powerfully challenge our view of God than experiencing years of seemingly unanswered prayer—as is the case for my nieces, nephews and many of you. I'm only six months into my journey with illness and my view of God has been threatened countless times. Many of you are years, even decades, down a very similar road. You wonder if it is actually leading anywhere or if you somehow missed the "Dead End" sign miles back.

Our view of God can erode like unplanted soil on a hillside. Let me be specific from my own life:

- I know that my view of God is being threatened when I struggle with songs I once sang with faith and ease. Some days these songs are now irritating to me.

- I know my view of God is being challenged when Bible promises that once held such hope now feel hollow or even hurtful. At times, the Bible has felt like sandpaper to my soul.

- I know my view of God is at risk when I don't begin to know how to approach Him in prayer. Some days my prayers have been reduced to little more than whimpers and complaints.

In March, I had my first opportunity to "preach" again. Standing behind my walker, with my voice unintelligible to many, I spoke briefly to our church family. Rallying all the energy and faith I had, I stood before our congregation and declared, "God is in this and God is good." Since then, thousands of people have watched me say that via video. I'm glad I declared it. I still believe it. But believe me: That faith statement has been challenged countless times since then.

In the end I don't know what to say to the barren wombs and broken hearts. I often don't know what to say to myself. But I do know what I refuse to allow in my heart, and I trust you will reject it in yours as well. I refuse to believe any less than what is required of us in Hebrews 11:6: "And without faith it is impossible to please God, because anyone who comes to him must believe that he exists and that he rewards those who diligently seek him." He's real and He rewards the earnest seeker. To believe any less is to not have faith. To not have faith is unpleasing to God and undermining to ourselves. To not have faith is to begin to self-destruct.

In a season of seemingly unanswered prayer, I'm clinging to the basics: God is real. God is good. This is about all I know.

I trust you will cling as well, even when the evidence seems a little thin. This is true faith. This is the challenge for every Christ-follower who has had to suffer. These are the most important thoughts you will think.

Keep believing,
John

$\mathcal{M}ay$ 15
A DAY AT SEA

My sickness began last October when I was away for the week on a study break. After a weekend of church services and meetings, I loaded my car with two large boxes of books and a cooler of food and headed to the Oregon Coast to stay alone in a home on the ocean at the kindness of a friend. Flu-like symptoms were beginning, but what could be better than solitude by the ocean to recuperate?

Throughout the week, my body ached and weakened, but my mind was clear and I made huge progress as I worked on my doctoral dissertation. The days flew too quickly as page after page were entered into my laptop, edited and then re-edited. Every once in a while, though, my writing mind would jump to a completely different theme than my dissertation, and I'd run with it for an hour or so—a poem to my wife, a children's book idea, a song. Such spurts of imagination don't always produce the highest quality material, but they do reveal what is in the heart and head.

This is the case for what I'm sharing with you tonight. I'm rather embarrassed by the song itself. It is neither creative nor strong lyrically. However, it reveals that I had a foreboding sense of uncertainty about my future. "Premonition" seems too strong a word. Yet, something within my spirit was already beginning to wrestle with the days ahead. At this point I had not seen a doctor or even considered it. I was convinced that I had the flu and I'd be okay in a few days. Deep down, though, other thoughts were brewing.

In spite of my awkwardness, I share this song not only to give another insight into this mysterious journey I travel, but perhaps to help you put some language to the journey you travel as well.

A Day at Sea

Verse 1
I'm tired of askin' the same old questions:
How long will this sickness last?
Will these prayer sighs of mine be answered soon?
Is there a better day coming?
Or when the next morning dawns
Will I be singin' the same old, sad tune?

Chorus 1
None of us knows where this journey will take us.
None of us knows where this voyage will lead.
None of us knows where tomorrow will find us.
This is why for Your grace we plead.
This is why for Your grace we plead.

Verse 2
I can't help wonder about my future.
My past I can't always shake.
But in the moment I come before You,
There is nowhere else to go.
I accept that You are God.
This is the wisest thing for man to do.

Chorus 2
Maybe I've been praying for all the wrong things;
Maybe I've been missing You all along.
Maybe I've been blinded by my own self
You've been singing with me the whole song.
You've been singing with me the whole song.

Bridge
I wish I had some certainty.
Life should come with a guarantee.
But the only thing I can clearly see
Is that much of life isn't up to me.

Last Chorus
None of us knows where this journey will take us.
None of us knows where this voyage will lead.
None of us knows where tomorrow will find us.
This is why for Your grace we plead.
This is why for Your grace we plead.

JPS/Depoe Bay, Oregon

Little did I know what kind of voyage I was really on. None of us do, for that matter. My only hope is to keep hanging on to the Good Captain. How about you?

Grateful for you all,
John

May 30
QUICK UPDATE

Well, my friends always thought I was a "few pints low," but the doctors have verified it. Now, three units of blood later, I am feeling a world better. I can't say that I feel great—but I certainly feel human again, sleeping better last night than I have in weeks. Thanks for your prayers.

And, a big thank you to all who donate blood. I know not everyone can, but for those who do, please know that this recipient is very grateful. Scripture tells us, "the life of a creature is in the blood" (Leviticus 17:11). I don't pretend to know the full ramifications of this concept, but I will say that the blood of three people was life-giving to me this week. I donated blood a few times myself through the years and know that it is never convenient, but now that I'm on the receiving end, I see the extreme significance. It is a noble thing that you are doing. It is a unique form of generosity. I celebrate it.

The bottom line is that I'm losing blood somehow and without someone else's, I'd be in big trouble physically. Your sacrifice sustains my life and gives me quality of life. Thank you.

Grateful,
John

TOUGH AND TENDER CAREGIVERS

June 1

Through the years my wife has used a household cleaning product called "Tough and Tender." It's named for its claim of being tough on dirt but tender on the item being cleaned. I'm stealing the name today as an appropriate label for some of my caregiving experiences.

For example, for a long period of time while in ICU, I was unable to move any of my muscles. This put me on the list to be the recipient of the services of the "Lift Team." Every two hours, every night, this team of two or three young men would come into my room, throw on the brightest lights, talk loudly, flirt with the nursing staff and with a "one-two-three," roll me to my other side and then jam some pillows under me to support me.

They'd leave as loudly as they came and didn't always remember to turn out the light. I understood the necessity of their work, i.e. protecting immobile people like me from developing bedsores and saving the nursing staff from the work of heavy lifting. However, it would have been nice if they could have showed some sensitivity to the fact that some of us actually like to sleep at 3 a.m. The Lift Team: tough, or maybe just plain rough.

Meanwhile, in ICU, I had a passing parade of nurses. In one of my delusions I believed that they were all part of an Eastern European plot to take over the United States—but that's a different story. Most of them served me very well, but there was one evening shift nurse I will never forget. To my knowledge, she was only there two nights. At the time I was out of most of my delirium but still had countless issues going on in my body—including a major skin breakdown caused by gaining upwards of 80 pounds of water weight. I felt like a beached whale bloating in the sun. Most nurses would give me a daily bath and care for my wounds, but this particular nurse was amazingly patient, thorough and gentle. I laid there in deep appreciation as she compassionately tended to every sore on my body and bathed me with the grace of an artist.

The mental image that came to my mind was that of Mary preparing the body of Jesus for burial (although according to the Gospels, Mary never had the chance to do so). I actually thought, *I wonder if I'm being prepared for my death,* and it wasn't a morbid thought. Her touch was not only healing for my body but therapeutic for my soul. "Mary," the nurse: tender.

Now that I'm home, I have had a few health professionals assisting me here. The two that come weekly are my home healthcare nurse (for wound care and general checkup) and my physical therapist. Both of them are a gift to me. Both, I am happy to announce, have somehow found a great balance in their caregiving style. They are my "tough and tender" team.

My home healthcare nurse is no one you want to say "no" to. When she knows something is necessary she has a gracious but firm way of getting it done. Meanwhile her compassionate and thorough care has touched my spirit while healing my body. As for my physical therapist, she seems to know just how hard she can push me physically, taking me right to the limit of what I feel like I can do. Smiling but firm, she drives me on.

I don't know why some people are able to find a balance in life better than others, but it certainly is a sign of maturity. I know that God has gotten a lot done in this world through off-balanced people, but I'm always appreciative to have people enter my world who have learned to not put all their weight on one leg (one argument, one position, one opinion, one attitude, etc.).

Some churches go to great effort to balance grace and truth. Many churches are grace-filled places but do not have the inner strength or conviction to speak the hard word when necessary. Other churches, as you well know, speak truth with great fervor but grace is only a word in a song. Churches that are places of both grace and truth are those that best reflect the Gospel.

Tough and Tender. Grace and Truth. Two examples of balance. Is there any weight-shifting needed in your life?

Those are my thoughts for today.

My love to you all,
John

June 4
HE MADE ME PROUD

Last night our son Drew was given the opportunity to speak for his high school's baccalaureate service. He's had speaking opportunities before, but this was one of the first times I had the privilege of hearing him. I know I'm his dad and therefore I'm biased, but I've got to tell you, it was good. His message was so appropriate for the senior class who find themselves in a place of transition. It occurs to me that there may be some of us who would benefit from the content of his speech as well. So I'm taking the liberty today to share with you a significant portion of his talk.

Over the past year, much of my life has been altered. As a result of hardships, core truths have faltered and many things that I thought to be reality faded away. The one truth that held strong through these testing times was the fact that God is good and that He loves me. I realized this while reflecting on this year, and I felt so lucky. I wondered what had held me close to God throughout these hardships—because I sure know it wasn't me. And after some thought, I realized that it was the community that I am in.

But now it is time to leave that community. It's time to go away from the steady support that I have had for my entire life—and it's time for most of you as well. We have in front of us an amazing opportunity: This is the first time that we as individuals have found ourselves completely in control of where we live, who we live with and what we spend our time doing. Also, for some of us, we have the opportunity to start fresh—to leave bad influences (and those people who drag you into things you wish you would not do) behind.

As we settle into a new place, it is so important that we are proactive about finding a healthy community—a body of believers, a body of people who care and who love. The worst thing that could happen is to let a community choose you—and they will—but the odds are that it will be a negative community. The phenomenon that bad influences are more open and inviting to newcomers than the church or other Christian communities has always bewildered me, but that is a different point. The odds are that they will be a people that drag you down.

Guys, when we go off to college, hardships are going to come. It is so important that we actively choose a people that will willingly support us, instead of taking advantage of our weary state during that time.

Without my family, my brothers and my pastors, I honestly don't know that I wouldn't have given up—given up on my faith, or even on life. With all my heart, I don't want to find out a few years down the road that one of us has given up—simply because we were too lazy or too embarrassed to surround ourselves in a healthy community.

Drew Stumbo

Wise words. Thank you for being part of the community from which I benefit. May you successfully find one as well.

Together for His Kingdom,
John

June 7
VERBS OF FAITH–PART 1

I'm really not trying to give equal time to both of our sons, but I am going to cheat again today and use some thoughts from our oldest son, Josiah. He and I were in a conversation recently about prayer and I was so impressed by his thoughts that I asked him to record them. He did so, and I'm including them today as our launching pad for a multiple-part series on the verbs of faith.

Here are our son's reflections:

When we pray, what kind of Father are we coming to?

I know one thing, He's a Good Father.

One aspect of His Good Fathering is that He loves it when we ask Him for good things, and He loves to provide them. We can know this truth for certain when we realize that this principle was one of the things that God sent His Son to clearly proclaim. He sent Him to tell us things like: "You may ask me for anything in my name, and I will do it" (John 14:14). The crazy thing to me is that He just leaves it there, that simple. As faithful stewards of the Word, we can notice that Jesus is talking to His followers in this context, but otherwise, there aren't any qualifiers. Jesus doesn't give any warnings or conditions. It's clear that His concern was that we ask, and we can't find much evidence for any concern about over-asking.

The image of a Father who knows how to give good gifts in Matthew 7 is another example where Jesus' concern was simply that His disciples ask. He tells them, (I paraphrase) "Even your parents, whom we all know are not perfect, know not to give you a rock when you ask for a fish, don't they? My Father is perfect! Don't you think He knows, all the more perfectly, how to give a good gift to His children?" And again He tells us to ask and then promises a response: "Ask and it will be given to you" (Matthew 7:7). Again, without qualifiers, conditions or warnings.

Mark records Jesus saying, "Whatever you ask for in prayer, believe that you have received it, and it will be yours" (Mark 11:24).

Probably the most striking example of this teaching was recorded by Luke. In Luke 11, Jesus tells a story of somebody who knocks on his neighbor's door late at night because he needs three loaves of bread. The neighbor is bothered at being wakened and does not feel much like helping out his needy friend. Then Jesus says something very odd. He says, "I tell you, even though he will not get up and give you the bread because of friendship, yet because of your shameless audacity he will surely get up and give you as much as you need" (Luke 11:8).

To me this story seems crazy! I try to read into it so much. I think the one clear thing that we can derive from this strange little parable is that Jesus wanted to make it very clear that we need not fear over-asking.

It's powerful to me that all four gospels contain very clear examples of this teaching. Jesus' invitation to ask and ask and ask must have made a powerful impression on all four of the gospel writers. A key part of our relationship with our Father in heaven is to ask for His Kingdom and our bread. And to think of the humility, the trust, the vulnerability, the intimacy of asking! It's a mysterious teaching for sure, but it sure is a beautiful one.

Josiah Stumbo

There's a lot of insight packed into those thoughts, but the primary take-away for me is that I shouldn't fear that I'm pestering God. He invites us to ask and persist. I confess I have been a fairly meek "asker" through the years, so I find encouragement from this scriptural insight that we are freely invited to ask and even challenged to persist in our asking.

"You do not have not because you do not ask God," James instructs us (4:2). I know that James goes on to warn us about praying prayers that are merely greedy in nature. But perhaps you are like me and have failed to see God as someone who invites our persistent requests.

"Jesus wanted to make it very clear that we need not fear over-asking," our son says. This is a new journey for me. Perhaps it is for you as well. Join me in persistently asking for those things you believe would bring glory to God.

More on this in a few days,
Your fellow traveler,
John

$\mathcal{J}une$ 10
VERBS OF FAITH–PART 2

A friend of ours married in her thirties and then was unable to have children right away. This led to frequent and fervent prayer. After a few years she began to wonder if she should continue praying for a child. When she talked to the Lord about it, she sensed God saying to her that she should continue to pray until God told her to stop. She now has children of her own.

We're in a short series on the verbs of faith. I'm sharing lessons I'm just beginning to learn and apply. This is why I was struck as I was reading Mark 5 recently. Here we find the story of Jesus healing a demon-possessed man. As you remember the man lived in a cemetery and was unable to be restrained by chains. As Jesus approached him, the demons within the man immediately recognize who He is. The demons beg Jesus not to send them out of the region but beg Him to send them into a herd of pigs on the hillside. He honors the demons' request. He "answers their prayer," you could say.

As the man is healed and as the demons force the pigs into the lake, the farmers rush to town and tell the story. This obviously produces quite a crowd. They too have a "prayer request." They beg Jesus to leave the region. Jesus does what they ask, gets into the boat and prepares to leave. As He does so, He receives a third request. This time it's from His newest disciple. The healed man begs Jesus to let him come along. For the first time in the story, Jesus says "no" and sends the man back town to give his testimony.

We serve this mysterious Christ who says "yes" to demons and "yes" to a frightened crowd and "no" to His newest, eager follower . . . all of whom "begged" Him. Fascinating.

Begging hasn't been on my list of prayer verbs before. Yet, my recent condition has brought me to this point. There have been times in tears that Jo and I have begged Christ for the "one touch." I know some of you have done so on our behalf as well. In Mark 7 we find a foreign woman doing the same thing: begging Jesus for an answer to her prayer. It seems that He is willing to reduce some of us to a place of desperation.

And so, I'm going to keep begging and I invite you to do so with me until I've received my request or heard His instruction to stop asking.

Paul, of course, is our example of this, as in 2 Corinthians 12 he prayed repeatedly for his thorn in the flesh to be taken away. In time, God told him his thorn was a tool He was using that would not be removed. So again, until a clear answer comes, I take my position as a beggar.

In complete dependence on Him,
John

June 13
VERBS OF FAITH–PART 3

When I titled this short series "Verbs of Faith," it felt a bit like an oxymoron. For many of us faith seems like a passive thing—something we have but not something we do or act upon.

In this short series I've tried to point out some of the actions that faith calls us to as described in the New Testament. In Part 1 we saw the wide-open invitation Christ gives us to ask and persist in our asking. He is extravagant in His invitation. In Part 2 we looked at the story of how Christ responded to begging. Begging is a word I associate with somebody holding a piece of cardboard at an intersection. Yet, this word is used repeatedly in Mark 5 and 7. As demons and people approached Christ, surprisingly, Jesus says "yes" to the demons and the unbelieving crowd but says "no" to His newest disciple. I am determined to take my position as a man holding a cardboard sign before the throne of God until He says a clear "yes" or "stop asking."

Today we're going to take a look at one more word, i.e. one more verb of faith. See if you can pick it out in the verses to follow.

"For all creation is waiting eagerly for that future day when God will reveal who his children really are. Against its will, everything on earth was subjected to God's curse. All creation anticipates the day when it will join God's children in glorious freedom from death and decay. For we know that all creation has been groaning as in the pains of childbirth right up to the present time. And even we Christians, although we have the Holy Spirit within us as a foretaste of future glory, also groan to be released from pain and suffering. We, too, wait anxiously for that day when God will give us our full rights as his children, including the new bodies he has promised us.

"And the Holy Spirit helps us in our distress. For we don't even know what we should pray for, nor how we should pray. But the Holy Spirit prays for us with the groanings that cannot be expressed in words. And the Father who knows all hearts knows what the Spirit is saying, for the Spirit pleads for us believers in harmony with God's own will" (Romans 8:19–23; 26–27, NLT).

Did you notice that three times in this passage we find the word "groaning"? First, creation itself groans as it longs for a day when the Genesis curse is completely gone and it is restored to its full beauty and expression of God's glory. Last, you notice the Holy Spirit groans for us, evidently in language that only the Father understands. How gracious of the Spirit to pray for us when we don't know what to pray for ourselves. If at times you've been at a loss for words in your prayer, it is not over; it has just been transferred to the Holy Spirit to pick up where you left off.

Sandwiched in between the groaning of creation and the groaning of the Holy Spirit is the groaning of the suffering believer. I find encouragement that Scripture validates groaning as a legitimate response to our current condition. This is an interesting counterbalance to James 1 where we're told to take joy in our suffering. Both are valid and both are necessary, but I've heard a lot more spoken through the years on "buck up, take heart, be joyful" in the midst of suffering than I have heard permission to groan. Friends, I'll freely confess that eight months into this journey, I'm groaning, and I find genuine comfort in the fact that I'm singing in a trio. I'm joining my voice with all of creation and the Holy Spirit Himself.

For some of you I just got a little too weird and mystical. But to those who have known deep angst of spirit in recent days, please know that not only do you not groan alone—you are in the best of company.

Verbs of Faith: ask, persist, beg and groan. You'll find more in the New Testament and in the Christian pilgrimage. Whining isn't one of them. God help us all.

Journey on,
John

June 16
VERBS OF FAITH–PART 4

The verb of faith that Joanna has been hearing from the Lord lately is "wait." To me, this is the most encouraging of the verbs we've discussed as it carries a sense of anticipation. It is also the most difficult.

David instructs, "Wait for the LORD; be strong and take heart, and wait for the LORD" (Psalm 27:14).

Not long after I was released from the hospital, our church videotaped Joanna and me. In the interview I quoted the verse immediately preceding the instruction to "wait." David declares in 27:13, "I will see the goodness of the LORD in the land of the living."

At the time of taping I didn't have any idea of the kind of waiting that might be required of me. At the time I thought I was on a straight trajectory of healing. I would see the goodness of the Lord in the land of the living. I was going to beat this illness! I didn't know any "wait" would be required.

The months that have followed have proven that I've not been on a "straight trajectory of healing" . . . from a human perspective anyway. Physically I have had many setbacks and am not as strong as my first month out of the hospital. Obviously, this is discouraging. My muscles are so sore and weak that the most basic of daily tasks such as brushing my teeth are literally a pain. My skin itches, my spirit sags, my days are long and my swallow non-functioning. On a positive note, the wound from the biopsy is healing very nicely and I sleep quite well at night (in between spits).

This journey of setbacks has brought with it the necessity to wait. I remember in my past life preaching that "God does some of his best work in waiting rooms," and I cited examples like Joseph and David—men who were trained for leadership through years of isolation. Little did I know that I would have the opportunity to live out my own message.

Joanna says that waiting best happens when we accept what today brings while holding out hope for a better tomorrow. I'm not there yet. I'm more like a child pouting in the corner than a man patiently waiting for the next train. Pray for us today, if you would, that God would give us the ability to wait with grace.

Grateful for all of you,
John

June 19
VERBS OF FAITH–
A POETIC POSTSCRIPT

Ask, persist, beg, groan, wait . . . this is the list of verbs of faith we've looked at in recent weeks. The list could be a lot longer—seek, knock and hope are other good ones. You'll find more as you search the Scripture. I hope some new insight has come to you in the series and that your prayers are strengthened.

Of the hundreds of people who are regularly reading this blog, the primary audience I am writing to is the significant crowd who know serious suffering, loss, tragedy or trial. I'm grateful for all who are reading, but it is to the suffering that I most directly write. In the process, I have promised honesty. Sometimes honesty in the midst of suffering comes across a little "raw." Such is the case today as I have tried to capture in poetic form some of my recent grappling with the verbs of faith.

Thank you in advance for reading slowly . . . picturing each scene as it unfolds.

—◦◦◦—

The Crossing

I stand at the intersection of Faith and Despair;
My cardboard sign reads, "Anything Helps."
I look upon every face
Of the motorists passing by
But am careful to not lock eyes.
I'm seen, yet invisible;
I'm known, yet unknowable;
I'm in the world, but don't feel a part of it.

The busy people are gracious as they pass.
My ears are full of comforting words;
My heart is full of sincere prayers;
My pockets are full of change;
My stomach full of food...
Yet I am empty,
A vacuum unable to be filled.
I find a park bench and a newspaper
And make it my afternoon bed,
Using sleep to forget who I have become.

I awake with haunting thoughts awaiting me.
I make my way to the dumpster behind the tavern
And resist the temptation to seek a few drops of solace
From the bottom of abandoned bottles.
I rip a panel from a Vodka box,
Pull a marker from my dirty backpack,
Make a new sign with a new message,
And go in search of a new crossing.
I'm on a quest.

I find a new intersection
Though I can't discern its name.
I look for Him in every passing window,
Wondering if I'd recognize Him if I saw Him.
He was a "Man of Sorrows," they say—
Quite a reputation for a king.
But what matter if I recognize Him

As long as He recognizes me.
I hold my sign higher, with more confidence.
"One Touch," it reads.
He'll know what it means.

I am the despairing woman seeking to touch His robe;
I am the fearful mother begging for scraps from the table;
I am the blind man calling from the side of the road,
"Have mercy on me!"
I am everyone whom God has humbled to the point of desperation.
I now know who I am;
I am a beggar,
And according to Him, therefore I am blessed.
"Blessed are the poor in spirit," the Sorrow-Man oddly preached,
"For theirs is the kingdom of heaven."

Tears come to my eyes,
Blurring my vision enough
So I can now read the street signs under which I stand.
I look and discover
I am at the crossroads of
Earth and Heaven.

$\mathcal{July}\ 6$
SEQUESTERED

Many of you are aware that my brother, Jim, is a pastor. Over a decade ago he preached a message I still frequently recall. In it he stated, "It is enough to exist for the glory of God alone." I believe he cited the example of wildflowers blooming on a remote mountain slope—to live and die never to be seen by a human—but to exist purely for God's glory and pleasure. I've loved the simple but powerful beauty of that truth. I've even preached it myself a few times.

Today I believe that God is calling me to apply this truth layers deeper in my heart than I previously imagined. Some of you will know very well what I mean when I say that our personal trial has sequestered us. Because of our illness or crisis, we have been pulled out of the mainstream of life's traffic and find ourselves on a lonely side road. Our lives, once a hub of activity, now stand almost silent like an abandoned building. Today I don't deal with a tenth of the details, decisions or people that I did a year ago, nor could I because of my health. My main interaction with people is via computer, an isolated mode in itself. I'm living, by necessity, a very quiet life. And, truth be told, I've hated it many days.

I, by nature, am an activist. My favorite conversations with people have been not in coffee shops but on fishing boats and jogging trails. My best sermons have been written after I've left the commentaries (important though they be) in the study and mounted my bicycle or wandered a walking trail for some active reflection. None of my hobbies involve sitting. There's nothing wrong with having passive hobbies (reading, for example). I admire those who have them. I'm just not one of them. As a result, this illness has caused a brutal shift in my daily routine.

"Let him sit alone in silence," Jeremiah lamented, "for the LORD has laid it on him" (Lamentations 3:28). I've thought of these words many times since my illness began. Jeremiah understood what it was to be sequestered. But, he continues, "No one is cast off by the Lord forever. Though he brings grief, he will show compassion, so great is his unfailing love. For he does not willingly bring affliction or grief to anyone" (3:31–33).

Existing for the glory of God . . . sequestered . . . sitting alone in silence: This is the path God has chosen for some of us at this time. May God grant us the grace to blossom on whatever hillside He has planted us.

Seeking to practice what I preach,
John

July 9
IN A PERFECT WORLD

As I've mentioned, I first began to feel sick during a study week on the Oregon Coast. I was fervently working on my doctoral dissertation at the time, but also had some creative juices flowing to write a few other things. One outcome was a poetic piece for my wife. With her permission I share it today in hopes that it will encourage a few poetic—or romantic—souls out there.

In a perfect world we would have enjoyed this sunset together.
In a perfect world my pleasure of watching it would not
    have been robbed by the absence of you.
In a perfect world we would always be together
and every day would close with you safely in my arms.

In a perfect world, I'd have no competition for your heart,
    nor you for mine.
We'd think each other brilliant and funny,
even if everyone else thought we were just foolish or silly;
it would only make us laugh louder at ourselves and love
    each other more.

In a perfect world, you would always understand me, and I you.
We wouldn't get that fearful or pained look in response.
But in understanding each other we'd better understand ourselves

for to know you would be to know me, for we would be one.
In a perfect world . . .

The sun has now fully set and early evening gray begins to
    fill the skies.
But as she set I noticed that it wasn't the sun itself that was
    so beautiful.
I don't want to speak ill of her—she is truly glorious.
But the beauty of the sunset was provided by the clouds.
Mysterious. Imperceptibly but undeniably shifting.
Clouds that could bring rain or be silently dismissed by an
    evening breeze.
Clouds that I would not have thought of making if I had
    created my perfect world.

Our relationship isn't perfect. We have our share of clouds.
But perhaps, if we get the right angle together,
We could see that they actually add the true beauty to our lives.

Like this passing day,
our lives will eventually be put to rest as well.
Had we had cloudless— "perfect"—skies,
they would not have been nearly as beautiful.

In this imperfect world, we will make a sunset together.
In this imperfect world, we will hold each other still.
In this imperfect world, we will not fear the clouds
but create a beauty that will linger long after our sun has set.

JPS
Depoe Bay, Oregon

July 12
A GOOD PRUNING

Now that I've relinquished my role as lead pastor, I need to make plans to move out of my office. No one is rushing me, but it's something I will need to do in time. In order to prepare for this transition, I've begun going through the files accumulated over the last seven years. Mostly I'm finding notes of ideas I had, some having been implemented but most now obsolete. "There is a time for everything," Solomon said. For years I accumulated. Now it's time to sort and fill a few recycling bins. This is a form of pruning.

Whenever I've attempted to prune a shrub or fruit tree, I know I've been guilty of not being thorough enough. I snip away at the fringes, but rarely have I really given a plant a true pruning. It's hard to imagine that I'm doing the plant good by cutting it back as far as a veteran pruner does. A veteran can see where the new growth will emerge and gives the plant room for growth. The work of the veteran seems severe to the novice.

My file cleaning is indicative of the season I'm in right now. There is a pruning going on not only in my files, but also in my heart. The Master Pruner Himself is at work. His cutting seems severe. So many of my passions, dreams, ministries, hobbies, pursuits and pleasures have been lopped off. I don't like this season—and I pray it is only for a season—but I acknowledge that a thorough pruning is a healthy thing. My hope is that new life will emerge where the old has been clipped away.

Some of you know well what I'm talking about. Activities you once enjoyed are now just photos and memories. Responsibilities you once carried are now merely files in a drawer. I don't think I can overstate how vital it is for me—and perhaps you—to view this as pruning and not just a loss. This is huge. It could have profound impact in our daily outlook. If I look around and only see a pile of lopped off limbs, I could despair. I *do* despair some days. Instead, if I can look closely at what remains and somehow look deeply into the eyes of the Master Pruner, I can believe that grace is at work. We are being prepared for new growth.

"I am the true vine and my Father is the gardener," Jesus taught. "He cuts off every branch in me that bears no fruit, while every branch that does bear fruit he prunes so that it will be even more fruitful" (John 15:1–2).

Gardener and Guardian of my heart, I entrust myself to You tonight. In the name of Jesus, Amen.

July 18
OFF-ROAD FAITH

It won't come as any surprise to you that Joanna and I talk a lot about my physical condition. She gets so excited every time I show some incremental sign of progress. She's so cool. What a bride! This beautiful exuberance counterbalances my Eeyore attitude. Living in my body as I do, I tend to focus on what is still not functioning rather than on what is improving. Prior to my illness I was always a "glass half full" person. Lately, it seems, I've been taking the less optimistic view.

In the midst of this, the one thing I don't want to do is limit God. "Without faith it is impossible to please God," the author of Hebrews instructs us. He goes on, "Because anyone who comes to him must believe that he exists and that he rewards those who earnestly seek him" (11:6). It is His nature to reward us—what a God! Yet, I'll confess that in the midst of feeling cruddy—while our trial continues—it is easy to doubt this truth. God doesn't act the way we'd expect Him to. He has His own timing and purposes. Sometimes He reveals them to us. Sometimes He doesn't.

Through the years, as I've preached sermons on faith, I've occasionally called people to have a "four-wheel drive, off-road faith." It's not enough to have faith when everything is sailing along. We don't sense much need for faith when life is on cruise-control. But when life takes a detour onto rugged terrain, faith is needed.

Deep down I know that God's not finished. He has more in store for me and you. As one of our faithful blog commenters has noted, "This is not God's last word" on the subject. But some days what I see and feel overshadows my faith. It's a good thing I have the wife I do.

Thankful for your partnership,
John

July 22

THE BLOG I DIDN'T PLAN ON WRITING

You may have noticed that I've been trying to stay on a three-day schedule—getting a new blog posted every third day. I don't always feel mentally or physically up to it, but it's been my goal. Last night I was right on schedule with another blog completely finished and literally one click away from being posted for the world to see. However, I had a check in my spirit. Something wasn't quite right. This bothered me because I liked what I had written. I thought it was one of the best meditations I had written in recent months. I wanted to post it, but my spirit kept throwing up flags.

I paused. Then God brought to mind a passage that I hadn't considered. It countered one of my main points. My blog entry was imbalanced, not taking in the whole counsel of God. What I had to say had some truth, but it was missing the fullness of the Gospel. A quick re-write simply wasn't possible because now I didn't have the clarity I once thought I had. I don't know if it will ever be re-written or if it even matters.

So instead of my carefully worded piece, you are getting what I've promised from the beginning: honesty.

And, you're getting an appeal to listen to what is happening in your own spirit. If you are a follower of Christ, the Spirit of God lives within you. He instructs, counsels, guides and teaches. You can expect, therefore, to have times when He gives us insight or changes your course. Listen for Him.

I don't have any secret formula for identifying whether the voice we are hearing at any particular moment is God's or not. I'm sure I get it wrong sometimes. But the pursuit of listening is a worthy one, an essential one. "My sheep listen to my voice," Jesus said in John 10. I guess He means that it's all about relationship with Him, i.e. that the more we know Him, the better we'll recognize His voice. This is the path I want to pursue. Thanks for joining me on it.

ONE SHOVEL AT A TIME

August 1

My thoughts today arise from two comments posted in the last blog. From Oklahoma City came the prayer, "Father, all my life I've heard the words of Jesus about 'moving mountains' as instantaneous. Yet in reflection I confess that most of the mountains in my life seem to be removed one shovel full at a time. You're the Foreman."

Yes, my friend, it does seem like God has handed me a shovel! It would be nice if God would pick up the mountain of this disease and get rid of it with one toss. But for whatever reason that He knows is good, this seems to be a "one scoop at a time" process instead. I do believe I am being healed of this disease, but it is happening incrementally.

I don't pretend to know all of God's intentions in this. One of the cool parts of heaven will be the ability to "know fully, even as I am fully known" (1 Corinthians 13:12). I do know this much, however: As we quarry our way into the side of our "trial mountain," we unearth gems and diamonds that we would not otherwise have discovered. And, as we haul one wheelbarrow at a time, spiritual muscle is being developed that can't be developed in any other way.

I know God could heal me in a moment. One-toss ("one-touch") miracles are exciting and have a purpose. I still pray for this to happen. However, I want to accept that in the meantime good things are happening, one scoop at a time.

A second prayer came from Iowa, "God, I pray an extra measure of joy and peace to pour down like rain on my dear friends today. Wrap them up and overwhelm them with Your presence and assure them of Your love. God You are our healer, still today . . . we ask for Your mercy to pour forth in release for John's body. . . . We love You, Lord, and we worship You while we wait."

Worshiping while we wait . . . what a great posture to take. It reminds me of Isaiah 26:8, "Yes, LORD, walking in the way of your laws, we wait for you." My paraphrase: "I haven't seen You come through for me yet, Lord. But since You are my Lord, I will say 'yes' to You and do what I know I'm supposed to do while I wait for You." In other words, waiting isn't necessarily a passive state but rather a patient, trusting heart.

Moving a mountain by the shovelful takes time. Patience is required. It's easy for the digger to get discouraged. Keen eyesight is needed to see any progress. It helps to worship while we dig. And in the process, as has already been said, diamonds are discovered and muscle is developed.

So, to all my friends who are in a trial that God hasn't yet removed with one toss, keep quarrying. Keep participating with God in the mountain-moving business. Do what you can today to make progress. And, know that someday a shovel straight from heaven will take the whole mountain away.

Pressing on with you,
John

August 4
PERSEVERE-HINTS–
PART 1

Say it fast five times: persevere-hints, persevere-hints, persevere-hints, persevere-hints, persevere-hints. Yep, perseverance is the subject of the day. Not that I'm an expert by any means. I'm only nine months into this journey—some of you have decades of experience—but I have learned a few things en route that I wanted to record in this manner.

I'm thinking about those going through hardship as I write. Some of these hardships are physical in nature, many are not. All of them, however, require the increasingly rare quality of perseverance. I've been reflecting these days on the subject. There is nothing flowery or theoretical in what follows—just very practical tips for learning to persevere through adversity. I hope you'll find this helpful.

#1 Praise

I start this list with one of the hardest but most essential keys to persevering. When life is going smoothly, praise to our great God can flow naturally. When life turns hard, praise becomes a conscious—and often difficult—decision. Do it. Daily. We have unlimited reasons to praise God for who He is. And, every day we can think of at least a couple things He has provided that day to thank Him for. Become an intentional "praiser" and you will be the first step down the road of perseverance.

#2 Elevate suffering

In our culture of comfort, we view hardship as among the worst of all evils. This view discourages us in our need to persevere through our trial. If suffering—as our culture tells us—is all bad, then we merely want to get out of it and will fail to learn to persevere in it. Instead of buying the world's message, get a Bible with a good concordance or cross-references and do a word study on "suffering." (Romans 5:3 would be a good starting place.) God's Word actually gives us the hope-filled perspective that suffering is a powerful tool God uses in our lives. Study the lives of heroes like Joseph, David or Jeremiah and discover how God used adversity to make them the men of greatness they became. Jesus Himself, the "man of sorrows," is a model, showing us that suffering is one of God's carefully chosen tools (see Hebrews 5:7–9). We will be more likely to persevere through suffering if we see value in it. God does. We would be wise to as well.

#3 Rejoice with those who rejoice

In my trial I've found it far easier to mourn with those who mourn than to rejoice with those who rejoice (see Romans 12:15). In fact, my temptation is to envy those who have reason to rejoice as they go on their cool vacations, celebrate their good news or whatever exciting thing is happening in their lives. However, something good happens in my soul when I choose to celebrate with others. It is a difficult and conscious decision, but it's one more healthy step down the path of perseverance.

#4 Sense your progress

As you take the kinds of healthy steps of perseverance we've already discussed, you'll start noticing signs of progress. Like a "newbie" runner staying faithful with some good workouts, we'll notice that our stamina increases. Be encouraged! We are holding together in the midst of difficulties that would have crushed us some time ago. Even if no one else notices or encourages us, let's take comfort in the fact that we've made it this far. We're developing a "suffering muscle" that allows us to endure more than we once could. As we continue to exercise this muscle, we'll be even stronger in the future.

#5 Employ every resource

Don't hesitate to use every resource made available to you. Sometimes in our low points we can feel like we're not worthy of assistance. If someone offers help, accept it. If someone attempts to give a word of encouragement, receive it. My call to us to persevere is not a call to "do it all ourselves." We need other people. Be careful not to manipulate others into assisting you, but accepting any helpful help (we all know there are some offers that aren't truly helpful) available to us is not only appropriate, but wise.

#6 Value affirmation

One of the great gifts that Joanna and a few others have given to me is an unsolicited acknowledgement that what I'm going through really is difficult. They have validated the legitimacy of some of my grief. Again, resist the temptation to manipulate validation and don't wallow in a "poor me, I really do have it bad" attitude; but when encouragement legitimately comes, receive it. And, perhaps some would receive this from me right now: To those going through infertility, unemployment, imprisonment, the infidelity of your spouse, insults from your own children, injury to your body, and on the list goes—it is hard! We're more likely to persevere if we don't deny (or magnify) the fact that this is a hard "tour of duty."

#7 Expect ignorance

Well-meaning people will say the most unhelpful things. It's okay. People outside of our shoes or wheelchair can't really know what it is like to be in our situation. Their well-intentioned comments will be more encouraging to us if we lower our expectations. Perseverers don't expect everyone else to fully understand what we're experiencing.

#8 Rely on what you know to be true, not on what you feel at the moment

Long-term trials become major testing grounds for our faith. Our emotions can make a mess of us if we let them. Tie down some truths about God and yourself and cling to them for all you're worth. Pray them. Write them. Post them. Sing them. Repeat them. Even shout them. Our emotions will scream against this behavior like howling winds. Our soul needs an anchor (Hebrews 6:19). Let the truth sink to solid, anchoring places.

#9 Eagerly await what is coming

Every day is one step closer to paradise. In a marathon, every mile has a marker. Often when I go to bed at night I picture having passed another mile marker. I don't know how many "miles" we will be called to run, but I do know that at the finish line is a God-filled, joyous, pain-free future. Our present situation is not permanent. Those who are absolutely convinced that Jesus will return and heaven awaits are far better equipped to persevere through our current trials than those who don't live with this hope.

Okay, that's enough for tonight. I'll be back in a couple of days with the rest of the list. Meanwhile, I pray that at least one of these points will prompt some healthy thinking and wise behavior as we learn to persevere through trial.

Your fellow traveler,
John

PERSEVERE-HINTS–PART 2

August 9

In Part 1, I gave nine statements intended to encourage perseverance in the lives of those going through trials.

Praise
Elevate suffering
Rejoice with those who rejoice
Sense your progress
Employ every resource
Value affirmation
Expect ignorance
Rely on what you know to be true, not on what you feel at the moment
Eagerly await what is coming

Let me add to the list. For those who are going through a trial, here are a few more tips on persevering:

#10 Humor yourself

It's easy to allow too much "severe" to creep into our "persevere." It's too common for me to have a sour attitude while others around me are finding humor in something. In my healthy era, laughter came naturally for me. Now I have to be intentional about it. Not everything in life is laugh-worthy, but some things are. Don't miss the opportunities when they come. The best perseverers even seem to create a few . . . and some of the best humor material is finding reasons to laugh at myself.

#11 Include someone else in your journey

You can't do this alone. You weren't meant to do this alone. Invite someone into your inner world of struggle. This is risky, I know. Vulnerability is a dangerous place to go, but not as dangerous as isolation. If you don't have anyone right now, pray to God that He will reveal to you who it is with whom you could be transparent without condemnation. For a season, this may need to be a professional Christian counselor.

#12 Never underestimate the scope of the battle

This is big stuff. Don't downplay it. We're involved in a cosmic battle. Satan seeks to "steal and kill and destroy" (John 10:10). He wants to rob us of joy, kill our dreams, destroy our reputation, ruin our ministries and on that nasty list goes. "Our struggle is not against flesh and blood" (Ephesians 6:12). There is more going on here than meets the eye. If the enemy can bring us down, it will not only be one more victory for him but also cause a ripple effect of discouragement for the body of Christ. Meanwhile our perseverance has the opposite effect. Press on. This is bigger than you.

#13 Take one day at a time

I know this is an old adage, but I've felt the necessity of it like never before. In the midst of severe trial, life can be overwhelming. One day is all I can handle. One day is all *I'm called* to handle. God will give the grace we need for today. The manna will be there again tomorrow. Just live today.

#14 Seek a long-term perspective

Some days are just going to be tougher than others. In fact, some days all of your best strategies for persevering will feel bogus. It's okay. Accept it. Not all miles on the journey are equal. Not every step will be forward progress. Don't convince yourself that you've failed to persevere just because you've had a setback. Don't let a bad day or two steal your hope. "Surely your goodness and love will follow me all the days of my life" (Psalm 23:6)—even the bad ones. You are being pursued by Someone who loves you dearly.

—◦◦◦—

Well, nine months into my journey, these are my "persevere-hints" to date. Perhaps they will mature or change if more months wear on. And, yes, in case you missed it, the first letter of each of the fourteen points "just happen" to spell out the title. I am a preacher, after all.

Hanging in there with you, blessed ones,
John

"As you know, we count as blessed those who have persevered" (James 5:11).

PERSEVERE-HINTS–PART 3 (GENESIS 39)

August 12

One of my favorite Bible characters is the Old Testament Joseph—as in "can't keep his coat on" Joseph. You'll recall that his brothers' jealousy caused him to lose his first coat and he soon found himself being hauled away as a slave. Eventually he wore the coat of the slave in charge of Potiphar's household, but he couldn't keep that one either. You remember the story, don't you?

Joseph, the top slave in the house, attracts the attention of Mrs. Potiphar—a woman who seems to be accustomed to getting what she wants. In her attempts at having an affair with the handsome young man, I find three types of temptations thrown at Joseph.

The first type of temptation is the direct assault, "Come to bed with me," she demands one day.

The poor guy was just going about his business when suddenly he is face to face with a temptation. This "direct assault" temptation happened to me in high school when I opened the locker door and someone had hung pornography inside. It's happened to you when you were driving and another motorist suddenly cut you off. It can happen in a thousand ways—we're just going about our business when suddenly we are face to face with an opportunity to act very poorly. You should read for yourself the wisdom and strength Joseph shows in responding to this temptation.

Mrs. Potiphar isn't deterred that easily however, and Type Two Temptation follows. Genesis 39:10 reads, "And though she spoke to Joseph day after day, he refused to go to bed with her or even be with her."

Unlike Type One—the one-time in-your-face direct assault—Type Two Temptations just keep coming at you. This is the temptation that doesn't go away. Day after day she is after him, trying to wear him down, pressing her point, flaunting herself, using her most flirtatious tactics. Joseph goes out of his way to stay out of her way.

If Joseph were a lesser man, he would have broken with temptation Type Three. We find it in verse 11, "One day he went into the house to attend to his duties, and none of the household servants was inside." I'm guessing that Mrs. P. has personally dismissed all the other servants, put on her best perfume and donned her most seductive outfit. Joseph enters, just going about his own business. It is strangely quiet. She appears. Wow, does she look good. She grabs him and makes her demand.

Type Three is the "no one will ever know, you can get away with this" temptation. You are home alone and the porn site or pantry beckons. You're in a distant city where no one knows you; it can just be your little secret. Type Three Temptation is powerful. As her hands clutch him, Joseph doesn't hang around to talk this time. He's out of there faster than you can say, "Better go shopping for another coat." And in her scorned little hands she's left holding all the evidence she needs to have him thrown into prison.

For a long time I felt that Type Three Temptations were the most difficult to overcome. The secrecy factor adds a dangerous component for some of us. Adrenaline flows. Reason flees. Trouble awaits.

And, I still believe this to be a powerful form of temptation, but tonight I go on record by saying that in this long-term trial in which I find myself, Type Two Temptation has become my greatest nemesis. The day-after-day nature of this battle is draining. There is no break, no reprieve, no time-out. Every day I arise to face the same challenges. Perpetual weakness and consistent pain have a way of wearing a person down. Like a stick of butter left out in the hot sun, I hold my form for a while but eventually am diminished to a puddle. God—usually through Joanna—re-gathers me again with encouragement, but, outside of a miracle, Type Two Temptation taunts me that tomorrow is going to look a whole lot like today.

I share all this with you for two reasons. First, it seems that temptation loses a little of its power when we see it for what it is. I pray that identifying temptations as these three types will be insight-giving and empowering for you.

Second, my heart goes out for all those who are in a trial that is not letting up. Day after day you face the same issue. Night after night you pray the same prayer. Tomorrow will likely look a whole lot like today and it is just plain hard. If this is your story, I invite you to join me in my efforts to be one who perseveres. We've been given a challenge; let's rise to it. New mercies await us each morning (Lamentations 3). Let's press on together.

Your sojourner in suffering,
John

"Blessed is the one who perseveres under trial because, having stood the test, that person will receive the crown of life that the Lord has promised to those who love him" (James 1:12).

CLAP ANYWAY

Runners have trails and routes they fall in love with. Silver Falls and Minto Brown Park are a couple of my Oregon favorites. Because of its location, I only ran it a few times, but high on the favorites list is Moran State Park on Orcas Island, Washington. The spring before I became ill, I had the pleasure of a long run through Moran. When I got back to my laptop I recorded the following:

What an incredible run: 22 miles, 12 deer, 4 lakes, 2 mountain-sides, one really kind God!

On my circuitous route, I happened to pass the same man twice. He was an aging man walking slowly. It was impossible not to notice that he had one fully developed arm and hand, but his second arm was a bare stub.

We exchanged a passing greeting on the first pass but the second time he congratulated me with a kind word and a clap.

I was humbled by his applause. I don't know his story, but I admired his spirit. Did he have a crisis—a normal life that tragically changed in a moment? Or was this a condition from birth? Either way it didn't stop him from clapping, and I was moved. One-handed clappers don't make much noise—but they sure do make an impression.

I don't know if I would have the character to clap with one hand. I'm afraid that if I couldn't clap all the way, I wouldn't clap at all.

But he clapped and my plodding effort was cheered on—spirited on. Somehow a quiet one-handed clap meant more than a marathon band.

Percentages are that I'll end life with both hands. Percentages are that I have a few more years to run—maybe even a few decades if everything falls into place. Eventually I won't be able to run these trails anymore . . . but I'm determined to walk when I can't run. And when you run by as I walk, I promise to clap—one hand or two. And when I can't walk, I'll dream. And when I dream no more . . . as my soul leaves this body . . . I will no longer need to dream. I will walk and run again.

"I am going ahead of you to prepare a place for you," Jesus promised. I think He knows me well enough to put my "place" on the side of a forested trail.

Well, little did I know that just five short months later I would no longer be running or walking the trails. I thought I had years—even decades—ahead of me, and maybe I still do. But my point tonight is that I want to lift my feeble hands and applaud.

I applaud the Stumbo Prayer Warrior Team as they take on the 197 miles this weekend at the Hood to Coast relay, and I'm humbled that you've named the team in my honor with promises of prayer as well. How cool.

I applaud all of you who are doing your best to keep your heart pumping by some regular exercise routine. A thousand things discourage us from staying at it, but we know we're mentally and physically better off when we do.

And, I applaud all of those, like my one-handed friend, who have learned to live with a hardship and not let it stop them from living a full life. The cheer, vitality, faithfulness and grace shown by those in our church's wheelchair section amaze me. Others, like them, have modeled for me that the spirit can be more alive than the body. I want to be like them.

You'll have to listen closely; but if you do, you'll hear me clapping.

A CHILD'S CRY: A SHORT STORY

August 31

I can't run—or do anything that resembles running. But I can imagine. Here is the trail my imagination led me to recently.

The trail was new, but the sounds were not. Jogging through a forest unknown to me, I quickly relaxed as the sound of my pace and pulse played percussion for the chorus of wind and birds.

I love these moments. The race of my own thoughts is replaced by the rhythm of my relaxed jog. The worry and confusion that often run circles around my mind become quiet. I can't distinguish if I'm breathing deep to catch the fresh air or sighing. Either way I am renewed.

On this day the very first buds of spring were starting to appear. The trail showed signs of the last grip of winter. Leaves long fallen, now well underway to becoming soil again, were matted along the path. Winter's winds had left mud splattered and branches down. The wind still had a bite of cold. But the sun was warm and the squirrels were busy, and the afternoon was mine.

I didn't think anything of it at first. I don't know how long I heard it before I noticed it. A baby's cry—yes, there it was again, the distinct cry of a baby. Somewhere through that thicket, toward the direction of the sun, a child was in need. I slowed to a walk to listen, hoping I had somehow been wrong. Louder now—still distant and muffled—but steadily came the cry.

How could . . . why would . . . certainly there must be . . . but I can't just ignore it. My mind leapt from thought to thought. I was standing still now. Alone. Listening. A vulnerable child was in the forest crying alone. I must do something.

Grabbing a victim of winter's wind, I began to slash my way through the brush. At first I could make my way at a decent pace. The woods were thick with shrubs and vines, but passable. Every few steps I would pause to make sure I was progressing toward the cry. It seemed to increase in intensity and so did my determination. I must find this child. I must help this child. She . . . (he?) . . . must not be alone.

Soon the density of the forest demanded that I stoop low and thrust myself through vines and under low-hanging branches. The cry continued—or was it something deep inside of me I was now hearing? Had I not been that child, feeling so often alone, wondering why there was no one to help? I wiped my face, not knowing if the moisture was sweat or tears.

On I pushed, deeper into the undergrowth. The cry—so young, so helpless—drove me further. Soon I was on my knees, passionate that this child would not be alone and that the forest would not stop me. I tunneled through, ignoring the scratches of thistles and the grab of thorns. I wondered, *What kind of cry is this? A cry of hunger? Pain? Loneliness? Anger? All of the above?* It is difficult to identify one's own cry, let alone that of another.

I was close now. Very close. The cry was louder and less muffled. By the skyline I could see that a clearing was ahead. The thickest of brambles now blocked me. I forced a trail through as I crawled on my stomach. The thicket suddenly gave way to tall grass. One thrust of my hands and I had a sudden view into the clearing.

There he was—dressed in blue with a little cap pulled over his ears. Nine months perhaps. Red-cheeked from the crying.

The trail I had been jogging evidently took its own jog sharply to the west. The child was secure in a stroller being gently rocked back and forth by a father seated on a bench. He never saw me, but I'll never forget his loving look as he quietly spoke loving words to his child.

I silently crept back onto my newly formed trail. The sound was not new to me, but I had not heard it for a very long time—the sound of my own cry.

—◦◦◦—

One of the key factors in redemption—the complete restoration of the soul—is a deep assurance that God is with us and has been with us, every moment of our lives.

September 9
WHO IS CALLING THE SHOTS?

This week I'm attempting to write a Bible study on Jeremiah 29 for our church. This is one of the better known chapters in Jeremiah. The persevering prophet writes a letter to countrymen who have ignored his teaching and now live hundreds of miles away as captives to Babylon. False prophets are telling the people that they are going to get to go home soon, but Jeremiah delivers the surprising message that they should unpack, settle in and build homes because they are going to be there for a while: 70 years to be exact. The chapter also contains the much-loved promise, "I know the plans I have for you . . . plans to prosper you and not to harm you, plans to give you hope and a future" (29:11).

I can't share the whole study with you today, but I had to let you in on a new insight I had into the text. Maybe you saw it years ago, but for me this was new. Verse one reads, "This is the text of the letter that the prophet Jeremiah sent from Jerusalem to the surviving elders among the exiles and to the priests, the prophets and all the other people Nebuchadnezzar had carried into exile from Jerusalem to Babylon." Straightforward. Simple enough. But notice what the text says just three verses later, "This is what the Lord Almighty, the God of Israel, says to all those I carried into exile from Jerusalem to Babylon."

Who "carried" the people into exile? Verse one tells us that King Nebuchadnezzar did, but, in verse four, God claims responsibility. I love this. From a human vantage point, it looked like Nebuchadnezzar was calling

---

the shots. But from the divine view, God is claiming to be fully in charge. God seems to be saying, "What you saw with your eyes was an earthly king marching through your streets taking you captive, but I want you to know I am the one who has done this. I am still in charge."

Throughout my illness, quite a few of you have been kind enough to send me books. I've appreciated this, although I'm not doing too well sending out thank-you notes. As I've been reading some of them, it's been interesting to see how respected Christian leaders have opposite views on this subject. One author leads a large church on the east coast. He argues very clearly that God brings hardship into our lives to break us in our place of strength because spiritual brokenness is so highly valued by Him. Meanwhile, from the other side of the United States and theological spectrum, another pastor of another large church debunks such a view stating, "When we allow sickness . . . to be thought of as God-ordained tools He uses to make us more like Jesus, we have participated in a very shameful act."

The east coast pastor teaches, "God orchestrates every circumstance that touches every life to accomplish his perfect purposes. There are no accidents, coincidences or acts of fate in this world." Meanwhile, from the west coast I read, "Not everything that happens is God's will. God gets blamed for so much in the name of His sovereignty."

Who's right? Well, maybe they both are. I don't know. The debate is almost as old as our faith and will continue until Christ comes back. I do like the balance brought by another author who said, "Suffering is both our calling and our curse." Hardship is part of our calling as Christ-followers, but it's also a part of living on a fallen planet.

Since February I have been saying in regard to my illness, "God is in this, and God is good." The timing and nature of my crisis were such that I could not believe this sickness is just some random occurrence. Something supernatural is at work. On the surface, it looks like an evil "Nebuchadnezzar virus" carried me somewhere I didn't want to be; but I seem to keep hearing God say, "I was the one who carried you there."

In His grip,
John

September 18
THE FINE ART OF
ASKING FOR HELP

Joanna and I had a big outing today: We went to the Portland airport to pick up her sister who is visiting us from Wisconsin for a week. In the past I never would have considered a run up to the airport to be a "big outing," but my perception of things has changed. What once was routine, now feels significant. What once was simple, now seems complex.

Take, for example, the routine act of getting out of bed in the morning. Like any healthy person, this once was a simple, one-step process. Oh, I'm not denying that sometimes I stalled the process for a good while—I can hit a snooze alarm with the best of them—but once decided it was quite basic: In one motion I'd throw off the covers and sit on the edge of the bed. It was that simple.

Now, with my limited mobility and strength, this is a multi-step process involving the following: The first task is to lift off the covers. With my profound muscle weakness, it feels like I'm trying to lift a piano. With great effort I pull-kick-wiggle-squirm the covers off. Next, with great effort, I attempt to roll to my side and get my arm in a proper position so I can prepare for a push-off. Next, I drop my legs over the edge while thrusting with my arms in hopes that I have sufficient momentum to get all the way into the seated position. And, oh yes, don't forget the grunts and groans that go with it. Sometimes it takes a few tries. Usually, to be honest, I just let Joanna help me. Yes, I can be a slacker in the morning.

I know there are many with worse conditions than mine who would love to have the ability to get out of bed on their own no matter how many steps it took, but I share this as a simple example of the fact that some of the routines of life have become more complicated.

So today we're at the airport. We found our way into the short-term parking garage and I told Joanna to go ahead as I wanted to take my time and meet her at Baggage Claim. We keep some bottles of juice in the van in case I need a little nourishment when we're out. Just before she left, I asked her for a bottle. She kindly handed me one and a syringe so I could pour it into my feeding tube. Then she headed off to find her sister. All was well until I realized I couldn't open the plastic container holding the syringe. Try as I might, I couldn't budge it. I beat it against the dashboard to try to loosen it, but to no avail. I grabbed my cane and found a middle-aged guy loading his suitcase into his trunk.

"Excuse me sir, but I'm not strong enough to open this. Would you be so kind . . .?"

This isn't the kind of interaction you have with a stranger every day, but he didn't seem to mind. He took the container from my hand, gave it a simple twist and handed it back to me. I thanked him and headed back to our van.

Next, I discovered that I was also too weak to open the juice bottle—a basic 10-ounce plastic bottle with a twist cap. A five-year-old could do it, but I couldn't. I twisted, I turned, I tried both hands, I covered it with a cloth to try to get a better grip. No luck.

Here we go again, I thought. I wandered back out of the van and intercepted a young man pulling a suitcase.

"Excuse me, but I'm too weak to open this. Would you mind . . .?"

Just like the first guy, without a word, he took it from my hand, gave it a twist and handed it back. I thanked him and we parted ways. I was two-for-two on finding helpful people—nice folk, these Oregonians. (Of course, there is also the theory that if you give a man an opportunity to show off his strength, he'll take you up on it every time, but I won't go there tonight.)

I'll spare you other examples of my neediness, but you get the idea: Without the help of others, there's a lot that wouldn't get done in my life. I'd be a hungry, housebound, un-showered, barefoot mess.

Asking for help is a skill I've had to learn. I didn't do much of it in my past life. I prided myself in my independence. I was often happy to give help, but didn't want to be in a position where I needed it. But necessity has driven me to learn what I didn't want to learn. As my rookie year of help-asking nears a close, I offer the following lessons:

#1 Every time I ask for help is an opportunity to humble myself. Words like "I can't do this by myself" don't flow easily from my lips. How about yours? They are good words, though. They are even words that heaven is waiting to hear. "It's not the healthy who need a doctor," Jesus said. He came for those who knew they were sick and in need of His help. I don't like to be needy, but if I am, I'm a proud fool to not admit it.

#2 Every time I ask for help is an opportunity to assess whether I really should be doing this for myself. As I've already confessed, Joanna helps me out of bed in the morning. This is something I could do, but it is oh so much easier with her help. In countless areas of life—most of them more significant than this example—I have to be honest with myself and discern whether I'm hurting myself in the long run by seeking assistance. I want to live out Paul's directive, "Whatever you do, work at it with all your heart as working for the Lord, not for men." Sometimes genuine help is needed. Sometimes I've just become accustomed to leaning on someone else.

#3 Every time I ask for help I give someone else an opportunity to do a good deed. Good works don't get us to heaven, but they should be the common practice of those who are headed there. "Let your light so shine before men that they may see your good deeds and glorify your Father in heaven," Jesus taught. We needy folk give other folk lots of opportunities for their light to shine and their Father to be glorified. This can be a very good thing.

#4 Every time I ask for help I have the opportunity to express gratitude. Some people in places of need get demanding. They expect and/or insist that others help them. I once judged these people, now I think I understand them. Nevertheless, it does no one any good to be demanding. It is neither helpful nor Christ-like. A healthy dose of gratitude makes any situation better.

Your fellow traveler,
John

September 21
PATIENT PATIENTS AND CARING CAREGIVERS

I had never spent a day in the hospital since birth. I never had a surgery or had outpatient anything or had any reason to spend time hanging around doctors. (Okay, I did stick my finger in the lawnmower one afternoon and had to get a few stitches in the emergency room, but I try to forget about that one.) I'd get a physical every few years, but other than that, I didn't have any reason to seek the assistance of the medical community. I hardly ever even took a sick day from work. Until age 47 and 11 months, I was as healthy as anyone I knew.

I say all this to admit I had virtually no experience at being a patient. I was a complete novice. However, after a seventy-seven day hospitalization, I think I can claim veteran status. And, as you know, those eleven weeks were followed by months of significant home care and therapy. The patient status didn't end just because I left the hospital.

I'm thinking of two groups of people as I write today. I'm thinking of all of you caregivers. Day after day, year after year, you take care of the likes of me. You're amazing. And, I'm thinking of *all* of us—everyone who will read these words—because like it or not at some point in your journey you, too, will become a patient. This is pretty much a given. The question is: What kind of patient will you be?

First of all, caregivers, you are amazing! You have made it your chosen profession to care for those who cannot care for themselves. This is more than a job; it is a calling. This is a high calling. You share with us your healing hands and hope-giving words. You coach us, caution us and call the best out of us. You give your best to us and then go to the next room or home and do it all over again. Wow. Thank you!

We know you are human and might have to stick us twice (like the phlebotomist did today) when it should have only taken one needle to draw the blood. We know that you won't like all of us patients the same, but we respect that you work hard to treat us all with equal respect. We know that you are people, too, with your own world of issues and hurts, but we appreciate the way you are able to set them aside to care for our needs.

Please remember that for many of us patients, this is a new experience. You've dealt with other people like us a hundred times, but for us this is something very new and different. We're worried and probably scared. We're experiencing discomfort and dealing with pain. We're not at our best. We're usually nicer people than you're meeting right now. It's really good of you to give us the benefit of the doubt.

For all the times we were too sick or self-absorbed to thank you, please accept our thanks today. Please know that we really do admire you . . . even when we don't know how to express it. The world is a better place because of you. Our lives are better because of you. What you do isn't easy, but we want you to know it's worth it.

And now a word to all of us. My favorite quote of the week is: "The challenge of enduring pain is not to become a pain to everyone around us."

Whether our pain is emotional or physical, it can easily spill over into our treatment of others. At our worst, we can fall into a mode of subconsciously thinking, *If I hurt, someone else is going to hurt.* This attitude can sneak out in our word choice and tone of voice. We may think we're hiding it, but we're not usually very effective at it. At minimum, our pain can bring out an irritability in us that is a pain to be around. We can easily fall into a demanding, insistent attitude that may get results, but it doesn't endear us to anyone.

It takes a special grace to suffer well. Few of us have the personality that naturally maintains a good attitude through suffering. But here's the good news: For every Christ-follower, the grace is there when we need it. This is the work of the Spirit of God in our lives: He gives us what we need when we need it. Many of you don't have the grace to suffer well now because you don't need it yet . . . but when you do need it, the Spirit will have a sufficient portion just waiting for you.

I have not been the perfect patient. I had to apologize for my attitude more than once. However, I will celebrate that I endured far more than I would have thought possible, and I want to testify that the grace was not my own. As always, grace was a gift from above. It will be there for you, too, when you need it.

Your fellow traveler,
John

September 28
GLANCING OVER MY SHOULDER: RANTING–PART 1

I feel so petty to admit it. I want to be a bigger person. I expect better of myself. Yet, I've promised you honesty, so here is the wrestling match of the night.

Through a variety of communications this week, I've heard of some of my peers who are traveling the globe this fall doing the work of the Gospel. They are speaking, leading, training, blessing, conferencing, strategizing and just generally doing the work God has called them to do. They are good men, godly men . . . and tonight I envy them down to their socks. I miss the days of doing what they are doing, traveling where they are traveling, preaching where they are preaching. You get the idea. I feel like I've been benched by the coach.

Okay, I know that I have a new voice and a new audience via this blog, and I don't want to downplay the significance of it. I also don't want an outpouring of sympathy in response to my honest spewing. Just let me process this with you tonight, and please pocket for yourself anything of personal application to your life. Back to my rant . . .

I miss what I once had: a strong body, a clear voice, clear thinking, open doors for ministry, etc.—I miss myself. What an absurd place to be! Meanwhile, the lives of those around me have continued uninterrupted or even improved circumstantially. They get to do what they love with people they enjoy in places they choose. Luckies! (I warned you, I feel petty in saying this.)

I took a walk by myself tonight for one of the first times since be-coming ill. With cane in hand, I carefully made my way along the nearly vacant sidewalks of town. It was a good time to talk to God about my jealousy. I didn't get too far in this whine session when I was reminded of the story of Jesus and Peter walking along the shore in John 21. Jesus is extending reconciliation to Peter and re-commissioning him to serve. It's a beautiful scene that reveals the loving heart of our Savior. The dis-ciple John admits to eavesdropping on the conversation, following along behind the two as they walk and talk.

At a key point in the conversation, Peter looks over his shoulder at John and asks Jesus, "Lord, what about him?"

This is not the conversation Jesus wants to have with Peter. Jesus basi-cally says to Peter, "I have My plans for John. What is that to you? You follow Me. We're not talking about him right now, we're talking about you. You, Peter, follow Me."

This is the message I heard the Lord speak to my heart tonight: "I have those men you envy right where I want them. That's not your busi-ness. You follow Me."

"Yes, Lord, but it doesn't seem fair. I . . . ."

"Quit looking over your shoulder at them. I'll take care of them. You follow Me."

Every runner who has had any degree of coaching knows that one of the great "no no's" of racing is to look over your shoulder at the runner chasing you. It's a huge temptation but is of negative value. Your best ef-fort will come from keeping every muscle thrust straight ahead. A quick glance over the shoulder has lost more than one race. It's also caused more than one Christian to stumble.

My best race will come from keeping my focus straight ahead at what God has called me to do right now. The comparison game won't benefit anyone. I must confess that it is my pride that leads me to envy, and envy leads me to dark places—places I really don't want to go.

This battle isn't just mine. Somebody in your world will likely have a better-paying job, a nicer home, an easier marriage, better health, more opportunities—you name it. Once you start the comparison game, it doesn't know where to stop. Our best option is to leave the lives of oth-ers between them and God, and keep our focus on the One to whom we will give an account someday.

I don't think Jesus is any more impressed with over-the-shoulder glances today than He was in Peter's day. I know He was kind enough to call my attention to it tonight.

Grace-filled Lord, I want to forfeit the comparison game. I want to be a "no show." May I know the pleasure of living my life with You and not wasting emotional energy comparing my life to others. You've given me my life to live. Thank You for it. May I live it well. May I live it with You. In Your holy name I pray, Amen.

October 1
SHOULDER: RANTING–PART 2

I've grown quite accustomed to being around food and not being able to eat it. It was hard at first, but having not swallowed for more than ten months now, I can now happily say that I've gotten past the point of gawking and drooling while others feast without me. Seriously, I've truly become comfortable being around people who are eating. I'm not sure they're always comfortable around me, but I do my best to assure them that it's fine.

Today, however, it got to me. It seemed like at every turn, I was encountering someone else enjoying food: an omelet, nuts, candy, chicken, pizza, Chinese carry-out, pears, a peanut butter snack bar, burgers, cottage cheese, CHEESECAKE, cookies, grapes, Doritos, more pizza, candy, more nuts, pudding, more burgers, more candy, ice cream cones, celery with peanut butter on top and a stream of soda running through it all. All that since I got out of bed thirteen hours ago. I try hard on this blog not to be whiner, but today I'm making an exception. I WANT TO EAT. I WANT TO EAT NOW. I WANT TO EAT EVERYTHING EVERYBODY ELSE ATE ALL DAY.

Now I know this is very unhelpful for you to read because you are already praying for my swallow to return. And please, I'm not looking for an outpouring of sympathy on this. You've all been very supportive and kind. As with Part 1 of this rant, please allow me to process this day with you without it coming across as a solicitation for sympathy.

Here's what I'm learning from this: Something interesting happens in the human heart when we suffer deprivation—especially when it seems like everyone else has what you lack.

For me, the deprivation of the day is eating. Let me suggest a list of the kinds of places you may have experienced "deprivation" in your life:

- all your friends enjoy a level of vacation travel that you can only dream of,
- you have a physical disability that keeps you from doing something you love,
- the results of aging bar you from experiencing some past joys,
- everyone else in your family owns their own home and you're still in a rental,
- all your friends got married but the opportunity never came for you,
- all your buddies keep climbing the corporate ladder and you find yourself stuck on a bottom rung,
- it seems that no matter how hard you study, you can't get the good grades your friends pull off without cracking a book.

You get the idea. *It seems that everyone else has caught a train for which we can't get a ticket.* Some of us have hopes that our point of deprivation is temporary, while others have to face the likelihood that we will live out our lives in this state.

The question arises: Can we be okay with ourselves, others and God when we can't have everything we want in life? It's bad enough when we can't have it ourselves, but to watch others enjoy the very thing we lack takes a special grace.

Without this grace we turn to ugly places. This sad list includes (but is not limited to):

- Being envious and/or bitter toward those who have what we don't,
- unhealthy fantasizing,
- burying our pain under an addiction,
- acts of violence,
- carnally self-medicating, i.e. trying to mask the pain of our deprivation by indulging in a sinful pleasure we would otherwise avoid.

Obviously none of these options are helpful in the end.

I'll share some specific, positive steps to take in response to deprivation in a couple days as I post "Ranting—Conclusion." However, for today please ponder this: The core question we must answer in our hearts is, "Is God in this or not?" To ask it differently: Am I alone in my deprivation—or is God with me? Do I face this challenge single-handedly—or do I face it with a Friend? Am I left to my own strength to face this hardship—or is there another power available?

Truth Check: Our church training kicks in at this point and we "know" the right answer. But knowledge that is only head knowledge does the troubled soul little good. We know that God has said He will never leave us or forsake us, but knowledge that is not coupled with faith accomplishes little in our lives. Do we have a soul-shaping assurance that God is in this, or are we really seeing ourselves as walking through this valley alone?

In God's kindness, I received this grace early in my illness. I received a confidence that God was in this mysterious journey. I often didn't hear from Him. I couldn't feel Him for months. I experienced a season of what many have called "the dark night of the soul." But, through it all I've had the grace of deeply believing that God is involved. I am not alone nor abandoned.

God is at work in my deprivation. Every time I sit food-less and drink-less at a meal is another opportunity for the plow of deprivation to dig a little deeper in my heart. Its blade prepares my soul soil for a greater harvest. Fallow ground becomes a field ready for the seed of God to bear fruit. If I didn't believe this, I would be angry at my condition. But, I believe that God is active somewhere in the shadows of this mystery. My experience is not in vain, and I don't walk it alone. His mercies are new—every breakfast-less morning. For that matter, His mercies are new every sunless, friendless, homeless, spouseless or jobless morning as well.

So, back to my food-surrounded day. Yeah, I became obsessed. I'll go to bed soon. It was healthy for me to write this and process what was going on in my head. Tomorrow is a new day, and I'll be fine. But I have to rejoice that my heart was taken new places today. The train station teaches lessons those with tickets will never have the opportunity to learn. The plow of deprivation reaches places nothing else can reach. It wasn't an easy day, but I'm glad I lived it and I'm the better for it. Thanks for living it with me.

Your fellow traveler,
John

October 4
RANTING–CONCLUSION

Well, I've ranted my way through the last two blogs. I miss the opportunities I once had and the food I once ate. I have hopes that good days of ministry and meals will return, but in the meantime lessons abound, and I don't want to miss a single lesson God wants to teach me along this journey.

As I've already stated, I'm very aware that I'm not alone in experiencing deprivation. It appears in many forms. The question for today is: "What steps can we take as a positive response to not having what others have?" To use a word picture from my previous blog, what do we do when the train has left the station and we're left standing on the platform?

A good place to start to is to simply admit to yourself that this is hard. Don't wallow in self-pity, but it is healthy to be able to look at a situation and know that this is tough stuff. Telling yourself "it's no big deal" can be dishonest and a quick route to denial. It's healthy to be able to say to yourself, *This is rough. This hurts.*

Second, remind yourself that you are not the only one in a trial of this nature. Reflect on 1 Corinthians 10:13: "No temptation [also translated 'test'] has overtaken you except what is common to mankind. And God is faithful; he will not let you be tempted [tested] beyond what you can bear." Don't fall into the trap of believing that you've got it worse than anyone else. This is neither true nor helpful. There are others at the train station if you have eyes to see them.

Third, as I said earlier, something interesting happens in the human heart when we face a deprivation. Explore what is happening within you. Where does your loss (which is usually on the surface/circumstantial level) take your soul (which lies deep within you)? What heart-garbage is your crisis able to remove? What god is it seeking to dethrone? What positive character quality is it attempting to build? What past wound is it identifying? What lie have you come to believe that it is revealing?

Suffering is an opportunity to grow. Some people waste this opportunity because they don't have the strength or courage to ask themselves the hard questions. In suffering, things are going on under the surface that are not present during good times. Grab some scuba gear and dive in.

Fourth, believe that God is good at redeeming these kinds of things. Deprivation and suffering become fertile fields for His work to flourish. He may not give us exactly what we want, but He's pretty incredible at making rainbows shine in very dark clouds.

I appreciate all the comments we receive on this blog. A recent one was especially meaningful: "All your experiences seem to be pebbles creating a path God is leading you on. Only He knows where it is going and His destination is precise."

Great picture! Great truth!

On my bad days, the "rainbows" are hard to find and the "pebble path" feels like a dead end. But, time and again, faith returns and says with Job, "Though He slay me, yet will I trust Him." Life may not be turning out as I expected, but I'm going to hang on to Him.

God doesn't waste our pain. He can redeem any situation, no matter how dark it may seem. This is who our God is.

Thanks for putting up with my rants. Thanks for walking this journey with me. Many of you have a difficult journey of your own. My heart goes out to you. I pray that these four points will be of help. May we together have the strength and courage to gain from our pain, grow from our trials and glorify our God every step of the way.

Walking on the pebbles,
John

Year Two

But while Joseph was there in the prison,
the LORD was with him;
he showed him kindness
and granted him favor.

Genesis 39:20–21

THE SETTING

As year two of the journey began, I still hadn't gained back any of the weight I had lost, nor had I regained my ability to swallow. The feeding tube, cans of medical food and spit rags were continuous evidences of my battered condition. With a "this is the right thing to do" conviction, I relinquished my role as lead pastor. In their kindness, the church leadership created a part-time associate position for me as I slowly attempted to get re-established in life.

Gratefully, with the faithful help of physical therapists, I graduated from both wheelchair and walker. A cane became my new companion. This change alone made me feel a decade younger. And, my spirit started to emerge from the "dark night."

Any positive tone found in my writings the previous year arose from a determined effort to not let despair win. Now, evidences of a positive tone became more common and less forced.

In the Pacific Northwest, low cloud cover can linger in the sky for weeks and even months at a time. Locals have coined the term "sunbreaks" to describe the momentary parting of the clouds and the reappearance of the "stranger in the sky." As Year Two began, I had no idea how long the cloud cover would continue to hover, but the sunbreaks became more consistent.

October 18
A YEAR LATER–PART 1

Joanna woke me up this morning with a cheerful, "Happy New Year!"

You might be thinking, *She's a couple months early, isn't she?* Actually, she was right on time, and I knew what she meant. We've now completed a full year of our trial. It was a year ago today, October 18, that I felt the first symptoms of my illness.

If all goes as planned, I'm going to take the next blogs to try to recap the key lessons we are learning since this saga started. There may be some redundancy with what you've already read in previous blogs, but I think it would be a healthy exercise for me to make myself think and write in these terms.

Flat on my back in a hospital bed so many months ago now, I told a friend, "I don't want to miss any of the lessons God wants to teach me through this." I didn't have a clue what they would be, but on this one-year anniversary it is time to do a "heart review." So, that's the plan. As always, thanks for joining me on the journey.

On our walk, today, I got a head start on this subject by asking Joanna what she thought were the key lessons God had taught us this year. She had a number of good things to share. Her first response was about experiencing God's faithfulness to be near to us at our lowest points. She cited examples of when she didn't know if she could go any further— she felt like she had hit absolute bottom—and as she cried out to God, time and time again He was faithful to meet her.

Throughout her life, Joanna has daily spent time in the Word, but never with as much hunger as this past year has created. One of the many chapters that has been meaningful to her is Isaiah 45. In it we find out we have a God who is able give to us "the treasures of darkness, riches stored in secret places" (45:3, NIV 1984) so that we may know that He is the Lord.

On our one-year anniversary of this mysterious journey, we together want to celebrate a God who is able to reveal treasures in the darkness. These secret riches, it seems, are primarily experienced by those who have had to dwell in the dark for a season. And, the most fundamental treasure we have found is that He is faithful.

A year later we are still claiming, "God is in this and God is good." There were some very dark days . . . weeks . . . okay, months for us. Yet, in no way could we ever say that we were abandoned by God. We didn't feel Him every moment, or hear Him every day or see Him at work in every circumstance. However, it is our honest testimony that He has been there every moment of every day working in every circumstance.

This is the God we love and serve. Amen?!

Your friends,
John and Jo

October 21
A YEAR LATER–PART 2

As many of you will remember, a year ago this week I was at the Oregon Coast at the courtesy of some friends, working on my doctoral dissertation. I actually had a great week of writing, but felt the whole time like I was battling the flu. At least this is what I told myself. Looking back I realize I wasn't being completely honest with myself and, as a result, with others.

I told myself I had the flu because I had never had anything worse than the flu before, so how could I now? I told myself I had the flu because I didn't want to think about having anything worse than the flu. I told myself I had the flu so that I could just go on with life. I told myself I had the flu because it was convenient. I told myself I had the flu because I'm skilled at self-deception.

If I had been honest with myself, I would have admitted that what I was experiencing were not your run-of-the-mill flu-like symptoms. I had a rash. This had never accompanied any flu I'd had before. My arms were swelling and growing weaker by the day. Tasks like teeth-brushing became a major effort. It was all I could do to carry my laptop across the room. The box of books I had easily carried in on Sunday night was an impossibility to lift by Friday. Weak and swollen arms don't usually lead the flu symptom list.

Meanwhile, from the neck up I felt fine: no congestion, foggy head, cough or anything of the sort. My thinking was very clear, so clear I wrote for at least fourteen hours a day and got a ton of work done. Other than a couple of very short walks, I never left the house once. I was on a roll, happily writing away.

When Saturday came, it was time to head home. Only one problem: I didn't think I could drive, especially because our car has a manual transmission. I called Joanna and we talked it over. It was decided that she and Drew would come and get me. This turned out to be a very good decision. I was far safer with her driving than my own.

Yet, another level of "safety" came just by her being there. You see, I suddenly couldn't pretend that all I had was the flu. It didn't take her much more than one look at me to reach her conclusion that more was going on than I had admitted. The whole week I hadn't talked face-to-face with another person. I can become quite a recluse during these study weeks. I didn't go out for a meal or into town for any reason. My only contact with people was by phone, text and email. In my isolation, I spent the week thinking what I wanted and telling people what I wanted without really being accountable. Such is the luxury—and danger—of isolation. Ninety seconds with my wife and my self-deception was exposed.

Now I hasten to say that in this particular instance, I don't think that my medical outcome would have been any different had I owned up quicker and gone to the doctor a few days earlier. The next two months of medicine were full of uncertainty on the part of many of the region's finest doctors. I'm not second-guessing my behavior from a health standpoint. My concern is actually deeper.

I, along with the rest of the population of planet earth, am prone to self-deception. Telling myself the truth about myself does not come naturally. It is a learned—a Spirit-taught—behavior. It is one of the first and greatest lessons of my past year. I haven't perfected the art of being completely honest with myself and others, but I have come a long way.

In the past, I excused some of my self-deceived thinking by reassuring myself that I was just "looking on the bright side." There was some validity to this at times, but often rather than "looking on the bright side," I was actually shading the truth. Like a tricky card dealer who knows what card he has buried at the bottom of the deck, I could easily "bury" things I didn't want others to know . . . or to think about myself. I could give you a politically correct answer and feel pretty good about it, but sufficiently cloud the story so that the raw truth was protected. Usually the primary one was I was protecting was myself. On a few, rare occasions I used this behavior in my pastoral ministry. On a fairly regular basis I used it in our marriage. I see it now and am not proud of it.

I've come to value honesty like never before—in others and myself. I'm tired of being a leader and husband who always has to put a shine on a subject to make myself look good. This was one of the blessings of my near-death experience and painful recovery. I didn't have the energy nor the will to play games.

I know there is a place for being careful about what we say. I'm not advocating unrestrained spewing in the name of "just being honest." But this place of carefulness must not be a place of hiding, self-protection or deception. I'm working on and making progress in being straightforward in my speech. Join me as I seek to join James who admonished us, "All you need to say is a simple 'Yes' or 'No'" (5:12).

Note: For a brief Bible study on the subject of self-deception, see 1 Corinthians 3:18–20, Galatians 6:3–5, James 1:22–27 and 1 John 1:8–10.

Walking this journey with you,
John

P.S. I'll be an outpatient at the hospital this afternoon. They are conducting a Modified Barium Swallow. This is the test to see how my swallow function is developing. I'll try to let you know the results in a few days. Thanks for your prayers.

October 24
A YEAR LATER–PART 3

Mike was there again to greet us. Mike had been my speech therapist back in December and January when I was still hospitalized, and he had given me my first swallow test. As Joanna and I made our way to the hospital this week for a second swallow test, I was glad to see that Mike was again the one administering it. He has a warm spirit and sympathetic nature. And, he remembered us . . . it's nice to be remembered.

The nurse seat-belted me into the chair, making some comment about keeping the lawyers happy. The medical staff put on their protective garb, and I was seated between an x-ray camera and a monitor. Before me were Dixie cups of barium in different thicknesses. If you have to have a medical procedure of any type the Modified Barium Swallow has to be among the simplest and least painful. While other procedures require probing and poking and other punishments, the swallow test simply consists of being spoon-fed a minty substance that shows up very clearly under x-ray.

As I tried to swallow the first liquid, the monitor revealed all. With incredible clarity, I could see the liquid pass my tongue, slide down my throat and promptly get stuck on a "shelf." My tongue activated the initial phase of the swallow, but that's where the process stopped. All the little muscles and movements required to close off the windpipe and open the way to the esophagus didn't function at all. Quickly, I was instructed to spit out the substance.

We tried again a few times with various viscosities and with my head in different positions, but the result was always the same. Mike didn't have to say anything. The monitor said it all. I had failed the test. My swallow was completely non-functioning.

I can't say I was really disappointed. It merely verified what I knew was happening (or wasn't happening) in my throat. Joanna came with higher hopes, so it was harder for her to watch.

Mike confirmed that I should continue my efforts at the tongue/swallow exercises all the therapists have had me doing through the months. With that "I'm sorry" look in his eye, we parted ways.

I'm writing in this series about lessons I have learned—or am learning—or have been introduced to but am too thick-headed to really get—over the course of this past year of illness. My ongoing struggle with swallowing brings me back to one lesson I've been summarizing in this way: "Accept today, but battle for a better tomorrow."

Now that I'm on the cane, we're sitting each week in a regular pew, but Joanna and I spent quite a few months in the wheelchair section of our church. One thing that struck me each week about the wheelchair congregation was their contented joy. Somehow, in spite of their infirmities (some of which were worse than mine), they had a lighter spirit than I did each week. I came to conclude that they had reached a level of acceptance about their condition that I had not reached.

At first, I resisted the idea of accepting my condition because I felt it was fatalistic to do so . . . that it was like giving up on getting better. My attitude was, *I'm not going to accept this because I don't want to be this way, and I don't plan on being this way indefinitely.* However, resenting my condition did me no good.

The healthy place where I'm trying to land is accepting the present while battling for a better future.

"Godliness with contentment is great gain," Paul taught his assistant Timothy. It is a step of faith to accept that even though I'm not where I want to be today, God is at work in my circumstances and He is good. To resent today and to complain about my current condition doesn't help anything. God is not honored by my resentment nor is my healing enhanced by it. Instead, as I submit myself under the hand of God for daily life—that is, choose contentment—I find a sense of rest.

What I needed to understand, though, and perhaps you do as well, is that to accept today does not mean that I must accept this as my reality for tomorrow. From my place of peace—acceptance—I can fight for a healthier future. I can bang on the door of heaven to heal me, work my hardest at therapy and take other positive steps to make tomorrow better than today. An attitude of acceptance need not lead to passivity or fatalism. Instead, it can be the springboard to a proactive effort and a new source of faith.

This is my lesson, but let me put on my pastor hat for a moment. Maybe this lesson needs to be yours as well. Put it together with the previous blog's message about honesty/self-deception. What of your life today do you just need to accept that this is the way it is? Your finances have tanked, a relationship is rocky, your emotions are raw, you have a bad attitude, or you are lonely. Admit it to yourself and accept that this is your reality today. But don't wave the flag of surrender as if there is nothing you can do for an improved tomorrow. Take a healthy step of progress. Keep turning in job applications, take steps to make amends, engage in renewing behaviors—you get the idea. From a place of acceptance for where life is today, work for a healthier tomorrow.

I believe God is in this kind of journey. I believe He strengthens us to take these kinds of steps. I believe He is honored when we lift our head toward heaven and declare, "This is the day that You have made. I accept it and rejoice in it. But with Your help and by Your grace, I will do something today so that my tomorrows will be better."

And, one last word, if this lesson doesn't quite make sense to you or you need to process it with someone, find an individual who has been in a good recovery program. Their twelve steps and serenity prayer have a whole lot more to say on this subject.

The journey continues,
John

October 28
A YEAR LATER–PART 4

They tested me for everything they could think of.

You may remember that during my long ICU stay, the medical staff there ran more than 100 tests to try to figure out what was happening in my body. Nothing was conclusive. As I left ICU over a month later, one of the leading doctors said to me, "Well, you stumped us all." Another commented, "I guess we'll just have to call it the Stumbo syndrome." It was a mystery.

When I finally returned home, I fully expected a steady recovery. Instead, I had a roller coaster ride for the next six months. At times it felt like I was climbing toward recovery and then I'd plummet again. By July I really wasn't any better than I had been in January. However, from July to the present, I've made solid progress. The most natural question to ask is why? What changed that I'm now improving?

The answer: It's a mystery. I do know that in July we kicked into a new level of prayer for a season. I know that at about the same time I had some changes in medication. I also know that during this time I became far more active in trying to exercise—getting out of the wheelchair on our walks and taking some steps of my own . . . feeble though they were at first.

So what is it that is bringing my healing? Prayer? Medicine? Exercise? My answer: All of the above. God is bringing about my healing in a manner that intellectually I can't attribute to just one cause.

All along God has been healing me in such a way that I can't give full credit to the medical world—or my own efforts. God has been answering prayer. God has been at work. I don't doubt this at all. But at the same time I can't discredit man's role in this either—the medical community or my own. As I've often experienced in life, this again is the mysterious interplay between God's work and human effort. I haven't felt led to flush my medicine and stop all therapy. I certainly will continue to request prayer. There is an interchange of divine and human at work in my body.

No one can tell us how I got so sick: There is mystery to it. No one can tell us exactly how I am getting better: There is mystery to it. But I want you to know that God is in the mystery.

This leads me to the lesson of the day: **If we will walk with God for a lifetime, we have to be willing to embrace mystery.** Those who must have every question answered and every riddle solved will struggle in life. They will either lose faith or distort their faith because faith by very definition implies that we won't be able to see or know everything clearly. God's use of mystery—not revealing everything to us to our satisfaction—is historically one of His most effective faith-building tools.

The command comes, "Leave your homeland, Abram. I'm not telling you where you are going, but I'll let you know you get there." Many of us have taken that same journey. We venture out into the unknown, trusting that He will lead us along the way. This is faith. This is the Christian journey. This is to embrace mystery.

Keep traveling.

On the path with you,
John

November 1
A YEAR LATER–PART 5

As I try to summarize some of the lessons of this past year, one place my mind takes me is to caregivers. Since I had been healthy for my whole life, I never had the need to experience caregiving or receiving, but my illness threw me into a new world—a world for which I am very grateful. And, no surprise here, along the way I developed a few opinions on the subject, some of which I will share at this time.

True caregiving is definitely an art. I would guess that during my seventy-seven days of hospitalization and months of rehabilitation, I have had at least 400 different caregivers. These would include nurses, CNAs, doctors, surgeons, therapists, phlebotomists, family members and the infamous "Lift Team" (the ICU guys who rolled me over in bed every two hours every night). All of them got their job done. Some of them got it done quite efficiently. I appreciate them all. However, among them is an elite class of caregivers who don't just get the job done, but do so in a manner that ministers something deeper to the patient than only taking care of the physical needs at hand. They aren't just doing a job; they've made it an art form.

I think an example would be helpful at this point. One of the benefits of being a hospital patient is that somewhere between 4 and 5 o'clock in the morning, you get to have your blood drawn. Oh joy. An early morning flurry of phlebotomy takes place as blood has to be drawn and sent to the lab in time for the results to come back before the doctors make their rounds between 6 and 8 a.m. It's a good system—for everyone except the patient who has finally fallen asleep. Waking up at 4 a.m. to see someone with a needle in their hand isn't the best way to start a day . . . but I digress.

For almost an entire week, I had the pleasure (I'm serious now) of having the same phlebotomist. I think her name was Lynette, but I could be wrong. I actually looked forward to seeing her. Now, I don't like getting my blood drawn any more than anyone else, but Lynette had the art of caregiving. She cared about me as a person. She cared about doing a good job, certainly, but she cared about much more than that. I soon realized that I wasn't just an object to her. I wasn't just a vein from which to draw blood. I was a person with a soul.

I think this might be central to the difference of being a caregiver who just gets the job done and a person who has a caregiver's heart. The former see the task that needs to be accomplished, the latter see the person before them. Don't misunderstand, I'm grateful for those who got the job done, i.e. meds were accurately given, sheets changed, biopsies and more biopsies taken and tested, etc. The medical community can work efficiently without the art of caregiving, but thankfully among them are those who do more than just accomplish their assigned task. They, somehow, have the ability to bless the whole person. If the human race were merely machines—soulless bodies—efficient healthcare would be sufficient. However, since we are spiritual beings living inside a physical body, having caregivers who truly care makes a massive difference.

Now I want to be the first to say that I don't think I could do this. It seems overwhelming to me to think of the emotional drain it must be to let your caregiving heart reach out to yet another needy person bedridden in front of you. With our modern medical practice, these patients keep coming in and going out like the waves of the ocean. None of them stays long, and as soon as their bed is vacant it is quickly occupied by another. I don't know how they find it in them to keep caring for continuous waves of hurting people.

Yet, I can testify that some do. I think of Nurse Nora, graciously tending to my wound, Nurse Jennifer patiently pouring meds and formula into my feeding tube, the CNA who was so kind as she gave me a long overdue shower, the Russian nurse whose tenderness was felt from my skin to my soul, my primary care doctor who gets that "I wish I could do more" look of sympathy in his eye when he sees me, and on the list goes. I can testify that there are true caregivers among us. As my wife, Joanna, has knelt before me a thousand times to put on my socks or put lotion on yet another outbreak of rash, I have been touched deeply by not only the physical act that she is performing, but the true sense of care that she is providing.

This level of caregiving can only come from a heart of caregiving. It's not a method that can be taught. It is a heart that must be caught (or, you could argue, given by the Holy Spirit—Heaven's Caregiver). This cannot be an easy heart to have. A price is paid by those who keep giving and giving of themselves. But, I believe that it is the price that Jesus Himself paid as He testified, "The Son of Man did not come to be served but to serve and to give his life as a ransom for many."

So today I celebrate those who have the art and the heart of a caregiver. Blessed are you, the true caregivers, for in you we have seen the Christ Himself.

My life is the better because of you. Thank you.

John

November 4
A YEAR LATER–PART 6

I told Joanna the other day, "I should get a bumper sticker that says, 'Spit Happens.'" Ah, yes, my sense of humor is rather twisted, isn't it? Yet, I've found this past year that while laughter can't take away pain, it does help keep our sanity in the midst of it. But humor in the midst of pain isn't my theme for today. My theme is—you guessed it—spit happens.

None of us gets through life without at least a few hardy doses of pain. Some of us escaped this reality for decades in our lives. Others didn't make it out of preschool before the onslaught began, but—young or old—hardship has its way of eventually finding us.

For whatever reason, I have spent the last year suffering in a public manner. Thousands know my story. To my great surprise, God has been using my public story in the lives of many who suffer far more privately. Many who have financial, employment, marriage, emotional or other personal issues often don't have more than a few people in their lives who know the real story. Largely, they suffer alone. These are the people most on my heart as I have written these blogs this past year.

My inability to swallow is just one of the many hardships I've battled this year, but in some ways it is the most constant reminder of my condition. Day and night the flow of saliva that refuses to go "down" but must go somewhere, tells me that I am far from well. I'm grateful for the saliva as I would hate to have the "dry mouth" condition endured by some, but I'll confess that I've grown weary of the constant necessity to spit. Some hours will go by with minimal and manageable need, but other hours (such as last night when I filled rag after rag) I am like an artesian well.

So I say it again: Spit happens. But I'm really not focused on spit in this essay. I'm merely using it as an example of the hardships we endure. For you it might be loneliness, unpaid bills, chronic pain, etc. And this leads me to a couple of lessons from this past year.

First, suffering enters our lives because we live in a fallen world.

As an old-time Alliance preacher used to say, "It is right that things are wrong in a wrong world. It would be wrong for everything to be right in a world gone wrong." Since humanity rolled out the red carpet to sin and welcomed it into our world, suffering is a natural consequence. I repeat: It is right that suffering is present in a world that is polluted by sin. Suffering is part of the world we live in, and no believer in Jesus—or anyone else for that matter—is immune from it. Jesus simply summarized it this way: "In this world you will have trouble [tribulation]." But then he adds, "Take heart [be of good cheer]. I have overcome the world" (John 16:33).

Second, suffering enters our lives because it is one means by which the work of God is displayed.

"Who sinned, this man or his parents, that he was born blind?" the disciples ask Jesus. The man was obviously physically impaired; therefore, sin must have occurred (the common rationale of the day). "This isn't about sin," Jesus responds (my paraphrase). "This happened so that the works of God might be displayed in him" (John 9:3).

I've had to ask myself repeatedly through the months: Am I willing to endure this suffering in order for God to be glorified in new ways in my life? At moments the answer has been a resistant, "No, I don't like this. I just want my old life back." But other days, by God's mercy, I've been able to trust that God has greater purposes than I understand, and if my little bout of hardship can be used for eternal good, then I will be a willing participant. As I said last week, I'll battle for a better tomorrow—this is not a formula for fatalism. Trusting that God uses these kinds of plots to write great stories, I'll accept today.

These lessons are not new to you or to me. I know we've heard these things before. But when suffering hits, they provide a foundation to keep us from getting knocked around too severely.

"For our light and momentary troubles are achieving for us an eternal glory that far outweighs them all" (2 Corinthians 4:17).

Spit happens. Glory awaits. Until then,
John

November 7
A YEAR LATER–CONCLUSION

As I write tonight, I carry in my heart two families who have had recent traumas. Troy survived twenty-two years in the military and the 9/11 attack on the Pentagon where he was working at the time. Upon military retirement, he settled into civilian life as a locksmith. Recently he was the victim of a senseless mid-morning shooting as he was fixing a car door lock in a parking lot. He leaves behind his wife and seven sons, the youngest of whom is only five. An older son serves in Iraq.

Meanwhile, a young couple I am close to went in for a routine ultrasound. To their great surprise and sadness, no heartbeat was found. The child they were expecting wouldn't be joining their home.

I haven't had to experience the kinds of losses these families have. I don't pretend to know quite how they feel. However, to a certain degree, suffering forms a fraternity. There is a fellowship among those who have suffered that is unique. Regardless of the kind of tragedy one endures, there seems to be a common bond formed with other sufferers. It has been a new and enriching experience for me to enter that "community."

One thing that I have learned in this journey—and the lesson I want to present to you tonight—is that *sometimes words have very limited value*. There are seasons of our suffering and grief when words are powerful tools and great gifts to us. They carry us on wings of hope. They bring light to dark places. They help us get out of bed and face another day. Words—Scripture, cards of encouragement, principles and truths, pithy quotes, powerful essays and prayers of faith—from trusted sources and sincere hearts pour fresh water into our shriveling souls. There are seasons for good words.

However, there are also seasons for silence. There are seasons when words, even the most well-meaning, feel more like arrows than gifts, salt water rather than fresh. The most beautiful promise not only doesn't inspire us, it mocks us. The most practical and helpful truths, rather than serving as a guide, feel like a sledgehammer.

For a few months of my journey this past year, I could hardly pick up God's Word. I did read it most every day out of commitment, but it offered no joy, hope, salve or healing. It was sandpaper to my soul. (Now my soul did need some sanding, but that's a different point.) I felt very guilty about this at first. I had loved God's Word for a lifetime. How could I be so cold to it now when I needed it most? Gracious people were sending me very kind words that just dripped like rain down the closed window of my soul. People prayed wonderful prayers for me, but I felt like an outsider observing from afar. It was not a season for words. The heart was simply too weary to receive them.

This condition gradually began to subside. In time, I was able to read a book, receive a word of encouragement and re-engage fully into God's Word. But I've come to accept and appreciate that one stage of grief for many of us is a "silent stage." Jeremiah, who was very familiar with the subject of grief wrote, "It is good for a man to wait quietly for the salvation of the Lord. It is good for a man to bear the yoke while he is young. Let him sit alone in silence, for the Lord has laid it on him" (Lamentations 3:26–28).

A few suggestions at this point. If you are reaching out to someone in pain and it doesn't seem like they're receiving your words, don't be angry with them or push your words harder on them. Your words may be good and fine, but your timing might be off. Nothing we can say will bring back the deceased loved one or make the pain of the moment any less. In time, the grief will turn to a new stage and hope will be found in words. In the meantime, your presence, appropriate touch, offer for a meal or another act of kindness might mean more than anything you can say.

And, if you are the person in grief, here's my advice to you: Save those words coming to you at this time—Scripture verses, cards, etc.—for the time when you are more able to receive them. Don't guilt yourself with an "I shouldn't be feeling this way" message. And, don't throw the words away prematurely. What you are experiencing will give way to a season when you are able to receive again. At that time you'll have a few words saved up.

A friend of mine made a journal list through her horrible crisis of all the ways God had intervened in spite of the tragic loss of her husband. Years afterwards she has found herself returning to those pages.

And, finally, please keep cracking open the Word of God, even if for a season you don't feel like it. The Spirit has a way of thawing and healing our hearts even when we are unaware of it. Fill your mind with good thoughts, even when they don't feel good.

There is a season for everything—even silence.

Your fellow traveler,
John

December 14

TOUGH ASSIGNMENTS

They didn't have an easy assignment. We celebrate them now, but it wasn't easy being them. If they could have, they would have written the script of their lives differently. Yet, they eventually discover that they are part of a much greater story line and it was not theirs to determine their own roles.

No doubt, Zechariah and Elizabeth had longed for children for a lifetime. Decades came and went with hopes unfulfilled. Disappointment became a familiar guest in their home. Yet, they clung to their God and lived lives that were upright in His sight (Luke 1:6). Their prayers for a family seemed to be met with silence, but this silence did not stop them from serving Him. They would obey and serve the One they could neither control nor fully understand.

With one announcement, their lives were completely altered. The angel Gabriel was sent to declare the good news: The barren, elderly couple would become the parents of the forerunner of the Messiah. Their decades of disappointment suddenly had meaning. They had been uniquely chosen for a significant task. The story line was being revealed, and they finally saw their place in it (Luke 1:13).

Certainly there were times of great joy. A child! A son! A miracle! What a pleasure and honor it must have been to raise this chosen child.

Yet, life is life no matter how "chosen" we are. Here they were, perhaps sixty or even eighty years old, trying to keep up with a strong-willed six-year-old. How many times were they asked, "Is this your grandson?" How many times did they think, "There is a good reason God gives children to most couples when they are still young. Why didn't He give us this child when we still had energy and strong backs?"

We never hear of Zechariah and Elizabeth in the Scripture after John's birth as recorded in Luke 1. What happened to them? We have no way of knowing, but consider the possibilities:

- Option One: They died at a normal age, thus not living to see the fulfillment of the promise regarding their son since John doesn't begin his ministry until some 30 years later.

- Option Two: They lived to a very old age and endured the incredible grief of knowing that their son died a sudden and senseless death (Mark 6).

I think Option One is the most likely. They were already "well along in years" (Luke 1:7) when the story begins. And, at some point as he grew up, John chose the desert as his home (1:80). It is my assumption that the couple didn't live long enough to see the fulfillment of the promise they had received about their son: "He will bring back many of the people of Israel to the Lord their God" (1:16). God gave them a major part in the unfolding drama of His salvation plan, but they disappear from the script well before the wonderful scenes of their son's baptisms and the Messiah's miracles. They had a part to play and then they passed from the scene.

So it is for all of us. If we become entirely focused on our little part in God's unfolding drama, we may become discouraged. Some assignments aren't easy. Some of us would like to re-write our part in the script. Yet, models like Zechariah and Elizabeth testify to us that it is possible to stay faithful to God for a lifetime, even when it doesn't play out the way we hoped.

Holy Lord, help me to remember today that I am part of a much bigger story than just my own life. Thank You that You have included me in Your eternal plan. I accept the role You have given me and ask for strength to carry it out well. Thank You that it all leads to something so very beautiful and glorious—eternity with You in heaven. It is an honor to be Your child. How could I wish for anything more? In the name of Jesus, Amen.

December 28
GOING WITH THE FLOW

I had a plan. I thought it was a noble one. On Christmas Eve Day I was going to write a Christmas prayer that I could share with my family as we gathered around the tree. I was also going to post it on this blog so that you could perhaps share it with your family as well.

I had the time carved out on Thursday to write the prayer. I was back at the local hospital for my third day of treatment . . . the five-hour process of receiving a very slow infusion of the best of people's blood. The treatment has been very helpful to me in the past, and I'm looking forward to the results of this round. Usually it takes about two weeks for me to feel the benefits.

Anyway, I was in my little outpatient room, arm hooked to an IV with laptop fired up and ready to go. I was alone, it was quiet, I had time. . . . I was ready to reflect and write a prayer. I'll spare you the details of what happened next. Too much specificity in stuff related to physical issues can be disconcerting. Suffice it to say that for the next few hours I was physically incapacitated and not able to write anything. I would need a change of clothes and a shower before the ordeal was done. I rallied enough to join my family for the Christmas Eve service, but by then the thoughts of a prayer were long gone.

Actually that's not quite right. I did have a Christmas prayer, but it had been reduced to "Lord, why?" and "Lord, have mercy." What I had intended to be a flowing, theologically rich and heartfelt prayer highlighting the significance of Christmas was diminished to a few-word sigh. When Christmas Day came, instead of having a prayer to share with my family, I read to them from a book. And, instead of sharing a prayer with you, my blog sat silent.

Why would I go from feeling fine all day to having almost instant physical issues when getting ready to write a prayer? Maybe it was all just coincidence—one of those flukes of timing that needs no other explanation than the fact that we live on planet earth. Maybe it was a spiritual attack—some demonic power gained enough influence at that moment to prevent a prayer from being written. Maybe it's proof that I really am allergic to Christmas after all—just kidding. Maybe, just maybe, God had something to do with it.

As with my entire journey this last year, I won't claim to know what was happening behind the curtain of human sight and insight—the curtain that blocks our view of ultimate causes and spiritual powers. My theology isn't cloudless enough to see my way clearly through those kinds of questions.

Meanwhile, I do know what a good and typical Stumbo response would be. Normally, I would say to myself, "I'll write the prayer anyway. It may be late. It may not be out of the romanticized Christmas feeling that I had envisioned, but—spit into the wind—I'm not going to be stopped." To repeat, I do think this would be a good response.

But it's not how I've felt my spirit (God's Spirit?) leaning these days. I'm going to save the theological musing for some other year. Instead, I feel like perhaps I'm identifying a bit with Joseph and Mary in the days preceding and following the birth of the Christ. I believe they had many "Lord, have mercy" moments. I believe they had to ask the "why" question on many occasions. As you reflect on the Christmas story as recorded in Matthew and Luke, pushing away the greeting card pictures from your mind, you have to acknowledge that it wasn't an easy season for the guardians of the Holy Child. A 100-mile trip late in the pregnancy, no room to stay in a town that was likely inhabited by relatives, figuring out how to care for an infant without the aid of a grandma, fleeing for their lives to become immigrants in Egypt. You know the story. Their rich theology (Luke 1:46) had to be reduced at times to humble pleas.

Maybe "Lord, have mercy" is a Christmas prayer after all.

I hope to talk to you again soon,
John

P.S. I trust you had a good Christmas . . . maybe even with some rich prayers. But if your Christmas had some hard elements, take comfort in knowing that you are not alone.

THE LAST HOUR OF THE YEAR

A year ago tonight I was still hospitalized. I had made some progress but remained attached to numerous machines and felt very poorly. It was a New Year's Eve I'd be happy to forget. Tonight, on the other hand, is one that I want to remember.

Our kids were all home, a rare but treasured gift in itself. We gathered around the table for games, complete with prizes (some junk, some of genuine value and a couple heirlooms thrown in for fun). Under certain conditions, prizes could be "stolen" from player to player. An heirloom of a notebook of Grandpa Stumbo's sermons became the most contested prize.

As the dad, what impressed me most this evening was the grace with which each family member treated each other. Genuine kindness and concern were expressed on more than one occasion. Tough competitors, all of them (I wonder where they got that trait?), but with an underlying grace. *A competitive spirit that is filled with the Spirit is a force to be reckoned with as well as being delightful to be around.* Such was my pleasure tonight.

Now the evening winds down for the married adults while the boys are getting Round Two started as our family room fills up with young adults for a prayer meeting. They want to usher in the new year with prayer and worship. Pretty cool.

Over the years I've heard many people say something to the effect, "Every day is a gift from God," or "I'm grateful to be alive every day."

I admire people who live with such an attitude, but I'll have to confess that many days this past year I did not have it. It's a strange thing to be a Christ-follower, completely convinced that heaven awaits our departure from earth. Many days this last year, I found myself saying that the "every day is a gift" sentiment was overrated. I would have rather been racing on streets of gold than limping my way across my driveway.

Yet, I've become content that we don't decide these things for ourselves. The timing of our departing "flight" is determined by Another. He alone knows when our time here is complete. He alone knows when our place is ready for us in heaven. He is the one who knows. He is the one who decides and it's not for us to try to take this matter into our own hands.

No, I haven't done so well at celebrating life every day it has been granted to me. Yet, I must say that I was glad to be here for this day, in the presence of these people for experiences such as we have enjoyed tonight.

So to my family I say, "If I can't be in heaven, I'm really glad I get to be here with you. You are cherished by me."

And to all of you in this blog community I say, "Until I fellowship with the saints in heaven, I'm thrilled to be connecting with people so faithful, gracious, wise, loving, caring and supportive as you. You have blessed me tremendously this year by your concern, comments, prayers and manifold expressions of love. You have truly been the body of Christ to Joanna and me this year. We are blessed to have you in our lives. We love you and appreciate you."

Thankful for the year past,
Trusting for the year to come,
Your fellow traveler,

John

January 9
TNTQ

Recently Joanna and I were having a significant conversation at our kitchen table. She was reflecting on some words of wisdom a friend had passed on to her a few years ago. Profound words. So profound I can't remember them right now.

As we continued to talk about her insight and our current life situation, Joanna wanted to know what profound words I had to offer. She wasn't putting pressure on me; she simply wanted to know if I had any insight on our situation. What had I been learning lately?

I rubbed my hand through my hair and sighed, "I guess we just try not to quit." Oooh, deep, John, real deep.

We laughed. That was as profound as I was going to get that night. We summarized my profundity even further: "TNTQ, Baby. Try not to quit!" It's become a little motto for us the last few days: TNTQ. It brings a smile to our faces as we take another step of life. God has been kind to us to give us humor in the midst of trial.

Then I received an email from one of my nephews, who ministers with his family among the impoverished and addicted. He relayed to us that one of the young men he had worked with through the years had committed suicide. This felt like a crushing blow to my nephew's ministry and a victory for Satan.

Yet, in the face of grief and loss, my nephew wrote the following, "But, it gives me more determination that this is an everlasting battle and it is raging. We cannot let up and we cannot give up, but rather should step up and be bolder."

Suddenly my "try not to quit" approach was called to take it up a notch. The real test of a difficult season of life is not just to see if we won't "let up" or "give up" but to see if we will "step up and be bolder."

In some very practical ways, I'm trying to step it up in these days: pushing harder in my physical therapy and attempting to re-enter and finish the doctoral program I had to put on hold fifteen months ago, to name a couple specifics.

Join me, will you? No matter what trial you're facing, it's certainly not the time to quit, and it may be the time to join my friend and determine to step up. The next level awaits. It might take a bit of a climb to get there, but I think we'll appreciate the view.

Your fellow traveler,
John

January 18
BODY AND SPIRIT

"I'm sorry about the source of that sigh," Joanna compassionately commented. "It's food-related, isn't it?" she accurately noted.

I had unintentionally let out a rather loud sigh as I walked through the kitchen and smelled the hot chocolate's sweet aroma.

I'm trying not to keep track of time, but it has been about fifteen months now since I last swallowed. Fifteen months of continual spitting. Fifteen months of smelling food I cannot eat. Fifteen months of pouring cans of "medical food" down my feeding tube. Fifteen months of feeling like an oddball in a world that eats as they meet, and eats as they walk, and eats as they drive, and eats as they watch TV, and eats as they get up in the morning, and eats before they go to bed, and eats when they celebrate and eats pretty much whenever they feel like it. And if they aren't eating, they have a cup in their hand. Some days the swallowing of liquid is even a greater craving than eating food. To have my throat quenched with a soothing glass of water, or grape juice, or chocolate milk or soda . . . ah, that will be a good day.

About once a day I chew on soft food and then spit it out. This prevents complete atrophy of jaw and mouth muscles and has helped lessen the insanity of not eating. However, there is something very unfulfilling about chewing without swallowing. There is risk involved as well. While nothing can go down my inoperable esophagus, I must take care that nothing goes into my windpipe. Meanwhile, there's something gross about spitting chewed-up food into a plastic container. And, it is maddening when my liquid feeding tube diet leaves me feeling unsatisfied, and I could chew all the food in our entire pantry and not alleviate the unsatisfied feeling one bit/bite.

On a happier note, I'm definitely feeling the benefit of the recent infusion treatment. I have been much stronger in January than I was in December. I'm back pushing new limits in my physical therapy, my voice is stronger and my general pain/weakness/crud has lessened to a more manageable level. For this I am very grateful.

"How is it with your spirit?" I was kindly asked recently.

I answered, "Most days, I'm doing well. I really believe what I say, 'God is in this and He is good.' However, I have some days that are pretty dark. Like the other day when Joanna asked me what was wrong and I answered, 'I'm just trying not to be angry with God.'"

And so it is. The battle of long-term illness takes place as much in the spirit as it does in the body. "In this world you will have tribulation," Jesus prophesied. "But be of good cheer," He adds. We will have to endure hardship, but a key to doing so is guarding our spirit (keeping a "good cheer") in the midst of it. Being convinced of the remaining portion of the verse helps, i.e. that He has overcome the world.

As always, thanks for journeying with me!

Your fellow traveler,
John

January 22
A WORD TO THOSE WHO SUFFER

It was one of those days. Physically I had taken another downturn. Days of battling to overcome my physical issues seemed to be erased with another round of the pain/discomfort/crud/weakness combo I've become so familiar with over the months. Joanna, ever sensitive to how I'm doing, looked across the kitchen table and sincerely asked, "How do you keep doing it? What do you cling to?" The kind look of sympathy in her eye revealed that she really did want to know what kept me going in the midst of suffering.

Without really thinking, I quickly responded, "That this isn't random, and it won't be wasted."

Now, as I've confessed before, let's be clear that I'm not a steady rock of faith every day. I can withdraw into a cave of discouragement and dwell in doubt as easily as most anyone. Yet, by God's grace, most days I really do believe this to be true: What I'm experiencing isn't by random chance, nor will it be wasted.

I'm convinced that your life and mine have purpose. The Apostle Paul certainly lived this way declaring, "I consider my life worth nothing to me; my only aim is to finish the race and complete the task the Lord Jesus has given me—the task of testifying to the good news of God's grace" (Acts 20:24).

When you study Paul's life, you realize that he could have and should have been dead many times. In fact, he probably was dead at least once (Acts 14:19). He lived with a longing to be in heaven but remained fully engaged on this earth because of a deep realization that he had a task to accomplish (Philippians 1:21–26). He knew there were a purpose, design and sovereign hand involved in his life. He knew that part of that sovereign plan was for him to suffer (Acts 9:16). I think Paul would say, "My suffering has purpose. It will be used by God and rewarded by God."

If I believed that this illness "just happened to happen" to me and that it didn't have any ultimate purpose or meaning, I would have despaired. I don't think I could have handled the level of loss I've experienced if I didn't believe there were major victories to be found in the process. But I have a recurring assurance that, while I don't like this journey, it has meaning and leads to a good destination.

I love the picture of Old Testament Joseph. He serves his unjust prison sentence faithfully while completely convinced that he has been forgotten (if not by God then certainly by the chief cupbearer). He was the kind of man who was going to give life his best shot, even if it was from a dungeon. Stories such as his encourage me that with our God, suffering isn't random or wasted. A purpose will be revealed; a reward will be granted. The purpose and reward may not be revealed at a time nor in a manner that I expect, but I believe this to be true for me and for all who will bear up under trial.

So, my word to you is: Carry on. Live another day to do what is yours to do, to love those who are yours to love, to serve those you have the privilege to serve and to receive from those gracious enough to give. Arise to another day you may not enjoy but can endure; a day you may want to forget, but that will not be forgotten by the One who delights in rewarding His servants. *Open the shades* to let the light in for another day . . . into your home, into your soul, into your relationships. Breathe deeply, pray humbly and give another day your best shot.

We can do this. He'll make sure of it (Philippians 1:6).

Your fellow traveler,
John

OF DREAMS AND HOPES AND FLOWER BULBS

I know a young woman who has suffered greatly in the last two years. She's working through her grief and fighting for her own recovery, but one thing she's finding elusive is the ability to dream again. She writes, "Maybe this experience is good in showing me that living in the present, focusing on what I have now is all that I really need. But I need dreams, too, don't I?"

When tragedy strikes, it throws so many areas of our lives into turmoil. We ask questions we never before asked, pay bills we never before had to pay, go to offices we didn't know existed, talk to specialists we had never heard of, face emotions we never before faced and in general get thrown into an arena that is unfamiliar to us. The foundations we had built our lives on start to show some cracks. The expectations we had for our lives come down with avalanche force. The dreams we had for our tomorrows now mock us. The future we once anticipated decomposes before our eyes.

Tragedy strikes—loss of income, loss of health, loss of relationship, loss of loved ones—and with it often comes a loss of hope. We were once people of hope, we lived with a positive spirit of expectancy . . . we would love, we would live, we would travel, we would serve, we would bless and be blessed. But now those hopes seem naïve, that expectant spirit seems unfounded. With old hopes dashed, why should I hope again?

I think that my friend's question is not only a valid one but also a very insightful one for anyone working their way through the ramifications of a major crisis. One component of being fully alive as humans is to dream, to hope, to anticipate. To have no dreams causes us to shrivel, to be less alive, to wither in spirit. But, with life so uncertain, with so many dreams already dashed, on what basis would we dare dream again? What rational person would dare dream fresh dreams while the old ones still mock us? Why set yourself up for such disappointment? Isn't it easier (and even wiser?) to not let yourself go there?

Buried in the soil of our yard are gladiola bulbs planted years ago. The bulbs are not attractive to look at, and unless we need to transplant them, they'll never be seen again. If you were to walk past this section of our yard today, you'd never know they were there. The only thing visible now is a patch of bark. Yet, in just a few weeks, as the soil temperature warms and the days lengthen, life will burst through the bark again. Slender stalks will reach for the sun and, in due time, another flower will burst forth, parade its beauty and display its Creator. It will last only for a season, but it was for this season it was made, and it is for this season that the long winter awaits.

Dreams are like flowers. In due time, they burst forth in glory. They speak of life. They reveal the Life-Giver. In due time, some flowers wither and die right where they were planted. Others are selected, cut, carefully arranged and put on display. A few are captured and preserved by a photographer's lens or an artist's brush. All will pass in time, but all have their beauty and purpose for the moment.

Not all dreams are to be preserved or fulfilled. That's not their purpose. If every dream we ever had came true, the world would be even more insane than it is today. No, the purpose of every dream is not to see something come to reality, but to see that we don't die before we're dead—to be so alive that our lives reflect the Giver of Life.

So, yes, my friend, I pray you will dream again, for to dream is to be alive. You've got a lot of life ahead of ya. Live it. Love it. Embrace it. And who knows, maybe one of those dreams will actually come into being.

I'll do my best to do the same. The world already has enough shriveled preachers. I don't want to be one of them.

Traveling and travailing with you,
John

February 22
A DECLARATION OF FAITH

God has given Joanna a new measure of faith this week. Her "hope meter" is running high again. It's such a rich gift to walk through life with a friend who is strong when you are weak and accepts your encouragement when they are down. During these long months of "recovery," we've often taken turns encouraging each other. Some days she's strong and I'm not. Other days we reverse the roles.

And, in all this I have concluded that it is okay to hang on to someone else's faith when ours has worn thin.

Our recent conversations have led me to write this declaration. Her faith strengthened mine. Perhaps now mine can strengthen yours.

One note: I view a "declaration" not so much as a prayer, but as a statement of what I believe. I'm encouraging you to use these thoughts to assert your own faith. I'd suggest that you read it thoroughly and then, if you conclude that it expresses your heart, read it out loud. Declare it. Speak it boldly. Faith is strengthened as words of truth are proclaimed.

In Him we live and move and have our being.

Christ is here. He is with us.
Christ is present. He is among us.

I believe we will be recipients of His grace every day we live. With David I believe that goodness and mercy will follow us all the days of

---

our lives. With Paul I rejoice that nothing can separate us from God's love. With Mary, I accept His divine plan for our lives and say, "I am the Lord's servant. May it be to me as you have said."

Christ is here. He is with me.
Christ is present. He is surrounding me.

I believe I will be a recipient of His grace this very day. I don't know if today will bring the grace of physical healing—or instead the grace to have the courage and strength to thrive in my brokenness. But I celebrate that both are acts of grace; both are from His good hand.

Christ is here. He is with us.
Christ is present. He is among us.

I believe that, as we have eyes to see them, we will encounter evidences of His grace today. He has no old mercies. They are ever new. He is never thwarted by evil, but can always bring good out of the worst situations. He is the God who can redeem anything.

Christ is here. He is with me.
Christ is present. He is encompassing me.

I believe that His grace will invade my world as I walk it today. I know that as long as I live in this fallen world, I will face hardship. But I also know that I can be of good cheer—I can live with joyful courage—because the One who has overcome the world goes before me.

Christ is here. He is with me.
Christ is present. He envelops me.

I believe that His grace will be sufficient through all of life. Even when my path takes me to the valley of death, I will have no reason to fear for He is with me. With that being settled, I can more fully embrace all He has for me this day, for I am alive. I am alive in Him.

In Him we live and move and have our being.

(For further reflection, here are the Scriptures that are directly or indirectly referenced in the above: Acts 17:28; Matthew 28:20; Hebrews 13:5–6; Psalm 23:6; Romans 8:39; Luke 1:38; Genesis 50:20; John 16:33; Psalm 23:4.)

Grateful to be on this journey with you,
John

February 25
THE QUESTION WE'RE REALLY ASKING

It is common these days to hear some form of the question: "Why do bad things happen to good people?" This question usually assumes that we know who the "good" people are and what defines something as "bad." My hunch is that God sees some of this a tad bit differently than we do, but I'll leave that point for some other day.

Meanwhile, I find it interesting that in the Bible people often asked the question in reverse, "Why do good things happen to bad people?" You can check out Psalm 73 and Jeremiah 12:1–2 for a couple examples of this.

From whichever direction you come at it, I think that the deeper question we're asking—both now and through the ages—is: "Why isn't life fair?" Whether it is the conundrum of the wicked prospering or the righteous facing tragedy, either way what we're really grappling with is the fairness of it all.

I've often been fascinated by how naturally the fairness question arises from the lips of small children. Kids, too young to articulate any significant morals, values or ethics, have an innate sense of fairness. You've noticed it. How many times a day is it shouted on some playground, "That's not fair!"? Even during diaper days, a child who can't yet say the word seems to have an awareness of injustice. When big sister gets some privilege the little tike doesn't get, it's not just jealousy that arises within him. Somewhere early and deep in the human heart is this demand for fairness, and if little "scream his lungs out" feels he just got ripped off, he's going to let you and the whole world within earshot know.

We grow up (hopefully) and (again, hopefully) learn to handle our disappointments more maturely, but the "fairness awareness" stays high. Somehow, for some reason, we expect life to be fair, and it ticks us off when it's not. We expect our court systems to be fair, and it angers us if they don't appear to be so. We expect the same from our police officers and the prices we pay in the store and the reporting we hear on the news. It shows up in a hundred ways in our lives, many of them far more personal and emotional. When a co-worker gets an advancement we were passed by for, when someone gets a financial break we couldn't get, when someone gets recognized while we get overlooked, when someone gets chosen "from the inside" and we didn't even have a chance to apply . . . you get the idea. Fairness frustrations are all around us.

Where did we get the sense that life should be fair? Where does this come from?

Joanna and I always worked at fairness in parenting. We'd keep track of how many presents each child would be getting for Christmas and how much money we spent on their birthdays so there would be a sense of equality. Many a Christmas Eve was spent shopping for the last gift because a kid was one short of having the same as the others. I'd argue that it is good to try to lead with fairness if you're a parent, teacher, government official, employer or in some other way impacting people's lives on a regular basis. Fairness is a good thing to strive for.

But I ask it again: Where did we get the idea that life in this world should be fair? Philosophically, I would argue that this is one more evidence for the existence of God and that we were created in His image. The fact that you don't need to teach a child about fairness—and that this is a universal characteristic—points to the possibility that there really is a supreme moral being who has instilled some of His nature into the human spirit. But that's really not my point today.

What I do want to say today is this:

1. When we ask a question, we sometimes stop too soon. We don't dig down enough layers to consider, "What am I really asking?" Questions should be viewed as quests to take our thinking and

our faith to deeper places. If one question leads to one or two more, rather than being frustrated, be grateful that perhaps you're getting closer to the core issue.

2. Fairness thinking leads to equation-making. Perhaps I just confused you. Let me say it differently. When I assume that life is fair, I assume that I can determine outcomes. For example, if this world were fair, good things would always happen to good people. We could count on it like a formula. Wicked people would never prosper. Godly people would always get ahead. If we did the right things raising our kids, they would turn out perfectly. Formulas. Equations. They don't work very well, do they?

3. The reason formulas don't work well is because this world isn't fair. We'll probably have less anxiety in life if we quit demanding of this world something it can't consistently give.

Is God fair?

I won't attempt an answer at that now, but I will say this, "He is good. You can trust Him."

May He give you the grace to keep your
head up in an upside-down world,
John

MARCH UPDATE

I live aware of the great blessing in life that I am prayed for by many people. What a gift it is that you have given and continue to give to me! I do not understand the workings of God and His desire to use prayer in His work—but, I do know that there is a definite and frequent intersection between God's involvement in our world and our intercession arising to heaven. God has used you in my life as you have sought Him on my behalf.

In light of the fact that so many of you are praying for us, I want to give an update as to how I am doing. I'm happy to say that I have much good to report this month.

New Winds of Encouragement Are Blowing

My spirit has been frequently refreshed in these days. After a long drought last year, the Word of God has come alive to me again in recent months in such a joyful and life-giving way. It has not always been true for me, and it may not be again in some future season God has for me, but for this season the highlight of my day is my time of prayer, worship and reading Scripture and selections from the saints. It's the best hour of my day right now. I'm reading through the Old Testament: a few chapters of history, one psalm and a chapter or two from the prophets. And, the saints are full of surprises. I praise God for the gift of this season of renewal for my spirit . . . all in direct answer to your prayers.

New Milestones Are to Be Celebrated

Okay, they may not seem like very big things to others, but for me they were physical and mental victories. First, earlier this week, I put on my own socks for the first time since becoming ill. Every other pair I've worn has been put on by a nurse or Joanna. It took a little "finagling," some pain and a couple of grunts; but in only a minute or so I got those little varmints on my feet. Happy day!

Then, while doing some neck exercises assigned by my speech/swallow therapist, I suddenly was able to do my first sit-up. It wasn't pretty. Don't ask me to do more than one or two. You might call it more of a "rock-up" than a "sit-up," but, hey, progress is progress even if it wouldn't win any contest!

March 15
WHERE I'M HEADING CHANGES HOW I'M WALKING

During this long journey, I have often struggled to find my own words to pray. I can't think of a time in my life when prayer has been so difficult as this past year. As a result, I've turned to some of the saints of old for help. Many days, when my words fell short, the words of the church fathers or Puritans ministered to me.

But, this week I didn't run across one from the saints that really struck me, so I sat down tonight to reflect on what was in my heart. Please don't evaluate this on the basis of good or bad poetry. It turned into poetic form as I pondered it, but my intent was to offer up a prayer. I know that the poetic form can aid some and distract others, but hopefully you'll be able to see past the form if necessary and agree with the heart.

You see, I've found strength many days this last year by remembering that this phase of life is transitional. My life will not always be like it is now. Neither will yours. Whatever happens in this life, as a child of God, I have another life to look forward to. For this I am truly grateful and again, strengthened.

Here's today's prayer:

> *One day the lion and lamb will nap together in the sun*
> *While the wolf and puppy lap together from the same stream.*
> *And all shall be at peace, and all shall be well*
> *For all shall be as one.*

One day the color of our skin will no longer be an issue
Nor the name of our kin something to be used against or for us,
And all will be equal, and all will be honored
For all will be made new.

One day we'll take deep breaths of Your glory
One day we'll know the wide breadths of Your love
And all will be joy, and all will bring life
For You have redeemed our story.

Today I travel the unpredictable path of this life
And experience the unavoidable wrath of this age.
All is not well, and all is not smooth
For this world convulses with strife.

But today I set my heart on the world of tomorrow
While I choose to start with You this gift called "today"
For You walk with me, and I walk with You
And I watch You heal my sorrow.

Expectation of my existence beyond this day
Gives me the courage to persevere for this hour
For in You I trust, and in You I rest
As in Your eternal name I pray.

Amen

Seeking to live with eternity in view,
John

THE FRIDAY WE CALL "GOOD"

As I've been attempting to reflect on this special week in the Christian calendar, my thoughts have drifted to Friday. I trust that this meditation will cause some reflection of your own. Let's be in awe together as we seek to honor our Savior this weekend.

The Friday We Call "Good"

When we wish someone a "good day," we don't wish for their death.
How then dare we call this Friday "good"?
If we had lived in Jerusalem that Friday,
*   we would have only called this a good day*
if we had been Christ's enemies.
The protectors of the status quo, the fickle mob, the demonic forces
*   and Satan himself—they thought it a very good day indeed.*
But those who followed Him, those who loved Him, those who
*   knew who He really was, thought it the worst day of history.*

Good Friday is good only if God Himself is truly good.

After all, what is good about betrayal, mockery, abuse,
*   beatings, torment and blood-thirsty violence?*
All of these were suffered by Jesus.
What good do we possibly see as evil is victorious,
*   injustice rules and hatred overpowers love?*

What good do we find in death?
Death is our enemy. Death is feared. Death is avoided at all costs.
Death is a tragedy, especially for someone so young.
How do we have the audacity to look upon something so tragic,
*   so heinous and horrific, and declare it "good"?*

Good Friday is good only if God Himself is truly good.

Everyone in our culture today wants to believe that if there is a God,
*   He is good.*
No one wants a "bad" God.
But the great weakness of our culture—Christian or not—
*   is that we want to be the ones who define "goodness."*
Health, prosperity, long life, harmony with others and the world . . .
*   these are all good.*
Anything less is not.
We will define the term, we will act as judge, we will determine
*   good and evil.*
We shall be as God.

But Good Friday is only good if the God of Good Friday is good.

Our reasoning continues:
Since we know what is good, we know that a good God
*   would only give us*
what we consider to be good.
Certainly if suffering or hardship enters our lives, it comes
*   from the hand of another, but never His.*
But what if we're short-sighted?
What if His definition of "good" looks to a farther horizon than ours?
What if we're blind?
Could it be that God is indeed very good—that He, in fact, is the
*   definition of goodness—but He is utterly different than we expect?*

Good Friday is indeed good because the God of Good Friday is good.
On that day when the sky became a shroud, the earth trembled and
*   the righteous wept, God knew what we could not:*
Suffering was necessary, bloodshed mandatory,
*   evil temporary and death the entry to life.*

The Definition and Definer of Good revealed that
  His power is so great, His authority so complete that even the
  cruelest of this world is redeemable.
The worst day of all of human history became good because
  God is good . . . good beyond our imagination.

May His goodness bring new hope to your suffering today.

April 15
SEEING SUFFERING BY CANDLELIGHT

Throughout my journey this past eighteen months, I've often confessed in private and public that I haven't been able to discern the source of my sudden health crisis. Some, whom I respect deeply, are convinced that this is an attack from Satan. Others point directly to the physical world of contractible diseases, excessive running (my ultra-marathon hobby) and the simple fact that we live on a fallen planet. It has been suggested that my own sin brought this about. And, while it completely goes against the theology of some of my brothers and sisters in Christ, there is also the possibility that God brought this about in my life.

In my time of quiet reflection this morning, I read Moses' review of the hardships his people had endured. The book of Deuteronomy is a recap of the history and law for the generation of Israelites who had not been born or were too young to participate at the time of the nation's refusal to enter the Promised Land the first time around. Forty years later, Moses gives the new generation a thorough review. In doing so, he provides an interesting commentary on what had taken place during those decades of wandering.

"Remember how the LORD your God led you all the way in the wilderness these forty years, to humble and test you in order to know what was in your heart, whether or not you would keep his commands. He humbled you, causing you to hunger and then feeding you with manna" (Deuteronomy 8:2–3).

Whatever the source of our suffering, I believe this chapter sheds light on the purpose of suffering in our lives. It begins to describe the good role hardship can play. Suffering has the potential of being a powerful tool in our spiritual formation if we will allow it.

Moses illuminates that hardship does the following (I picture him lighting four "candles" for us):

Candle #1: Suffering Humbles (Deuteronomy 8:2)

Anyone who has ever had to use a cane, haul around a walker or succumb to a wheelchair knows the humbling nature of needing these aids. Anyone who has had a family member who can no longer function in society due to psychological reasons knows the humbling nature of these trials. Anyone who has had to receive unemployment knows the humbling power of hardship.

I am not saying that the hardship itself is good. However, the Bible does teach us that humility is good. And, much to our dismay, hardship is a paved path to humility.

Candle #2: Suffering Reveals (Deuteronomy 8:2)

Moses instructs the people that God allowed them to undergo the hardships they endured to test them . . . to reveal what was in their hearts and to see whether or not they would keep His commandments when things weren't easy.

Like it or not, suffering not only shapes us into who we are becoming, but also reveals who we truly are. Many a professing Christ-follower has bailed on Him when things became difficult. When the prayer wasn't answered the way they wanted it to be answered, they blamed God and walked away. Meanwhile, others with equally difficult circumstances threw themselves in utter dependence upon the only One who could save them . . . whether He remained silent or not. Suffering reveals what we—and our faith—are made of.

Candle #3: Suffering Teaches (Deuteronomy 8:3)

Moses explains to the people that the daily meal of manna for the last four decades was also an object lesson. It is here that Moses gives the famous words: "to teach you that man does not live on bread alone but on every word that comes from the mouth of the LORD." There was a lesson leavened into their daily bread.

Every trial is a trail to a truth God wants to teach us. Some lessons in life cannot be learned in any other manner. It's a trail none of us want to travel—a school none of us wants to attend—but the lessons are rich and life-changing.

Candle #4: Suffering Disciplines (Deuteronomy 8:5)

Moses summarizes by telling the people, "Know then in your heart that as a man disciplines his son, so the LORD your God disciplines you." The author of Hebrews expands on this thought by instructing us to "endure hardship as discipline" (Hebrews 12:7).

It is unlikely that in this lifetime we will know with certainty the source of all our suffering. However, we can also know that it is an ideal training ground for righteousness. Our Heavenly Father, the loving parent, sees who we can become. Like any child, we need carefully applied discipline to help us become all He intends for us to be. Without discipline, no child fully matures. Trust the Father, the perfect parent, to lead us on a wise path to maturity.

By no means is this a complete list of the reasons for and uses of suffering. Much more could be said. However, I believe Moses' "candles" are as good a starting point as any I've found.

Final Word of Caution

Please do not forward this to someone who is new in a crisis. I was not ready to receive this a year ago. Suffering can't be fast forwarded. Early in suffering people may think they want answers and explanations, but what they really need is comfort and support. They need a season to grieve. They need to be given permission to ask hard questions without receiving attempted answers.

Please remember the context for these thoughts: Moses was explaining these truths to people forty years into a hard journey. They were not new acquaintances with suffering. They were veterans. Too often, in our efforts to help hurting people, we attempt to bring a premature closure to their suffering. This is a mistake. It can be very hurtful.

I've said it before: Grief is not a speed sport. Grief must be allowed to wander around the mysterious shafts and canyons of our heart. Its trek is usually best taken in the dark. But in time, the human heart is ready for light to shine again. Insights such as those provided by Moses provide darkness-piercing light and announce that a new era of healing is coming.

So, do feel free to share these thoughts with others—not like an unthinking night nurse throwing on all the light switches at once—but as a friend quietly lighting one candle at a time.

April 22
REENTRY

Joanna and I had the privilege of attending the annual district conference for the C&MA in the Pacific Northwest the last few days up in Portland. After eighteen months of being out of circulation with all of these pastors and leaders, it was good to be with them again. It was good to be one of them again. Our district superintendent, Matt Boda, even gave me the privilege of preaching for the closing service. I appreciated the theme of the event (and tried to speak to the theme, at least loosely): "We are an alliance of churches and leaders engaging in the life and mission of Jesus."

Please don't miss the significance of this, *I had the privilege of preaching at a pastors' conference this week!* I'm so grateful that, in answer to your prayers, I am now strong enough to be involved in this event. Other than missing out on the meals (due to my inability to swallow), I was a full participant . . . something I only dreamed of a year ago. Last year at this time I was spending my days in my chair at home, feeling absolutely ugly in most every way. A wheelchair was my main mode of transportation. I had only about a good hour or two a day to get anything done and then I'd crash again. Now my stamina is actually quite good.

I try to record and remind myself of these milestones from time to time because otherwise I get discouraged by what I still can't do, eat or be. Maybe you've found some ways to do the same in your life.

Today I want to share with you one point from the sermon I preached to the pastors.

I've been reflecting on Psalm 105:18–19, "They bruised his [Joseph] feet with shackles, his neck was put in irons, till what he foretold came to pass, till the word of the Lord proved him true."

The very word that Joseph had spoken—the word that he knew he had heard from God—became the same word that tested him. Being sold by his brothers into slavery had to be crushing in itself, but exponentially adding to its harshness was the fact that he had heard from God that he would live an utterly different life. He had dreamed and believed that he would be a significant leader. Now he's fettered and yoked.

As he's marched through the desert sands, his own "sermon" mocks him. I confessed to the audience at the conference that in my ordeal (miniscule compared to Joseph's) I've experienced the same. I've declared repeatedly that "God is in this and He is good." Yet, I have dark days when I can't see the goodness of God. My own message mocks me. I'm tested by my own words. This is part of the discipleship journey. This is part of God's training. This also gives one pause about what one preaches, as I'm increasingly aware that I might have to live out the words I speak in deeper ways.

Thanks again for your ongoing love and prayers. It means so much to not be on this journey alone. You have been a great help to me. Somehow, someway, I hope my journey is helping you as well. If we have to be in these bodies on this planet, we might as well help each other along the way!

Your traveling companion,
John

April 27
REJOICE WITH ME

There is much more of this story to be told, but for tonight let me quickly tell of our reason for celebration: I swallowed today! I still can barely believe it.

For a guy who hasn't eaten, had a drink or swallowed since the Bush administration, this is big news for praise. For thousands of you, who—for almost a year and a half—have prayed for this moment, this is a huge "Thank You, Jesus!"

Let me back up and give to you a few snapshots of our lives prior to this miracle.

Saturday: Joanna and I sat with some friends in a coffee shop sharing great memories, stories and laughs. What we couldn't share were the beverage and cookie. As they sipped and munched, I poured three cans of formula down my tube . . . my normal routine.

Sunday: A friend had Joanna and me over for lunch. It was a very pleasant event. The conversation was sweet, but I'll just have to take their word for the taste of the food. In her kindness, and as an act of faith, the hostess set a place for me at the table and stated, "I know you can't swallow, but I thought that maybe today would be the day you could." She was being thoughtful and full of faith, but I thought inwardly, *Today isn't going to be the day. I don't know if there will be that day. I know I'll eat in heaven, but I don't know if I'll ever eat again on this planet.*

Monday: Joanna kindly bought me a McDonald's ice cream sundae. It was fun to suck on it and feel its cold sweetness melt in my mouth, but none of it went down my throat. As always, I spit it back into a cup.

Tuesday (today): I woke up to a common sight: a mound of Kleenex on and next to my bed—evidence of another night of spit-interrupted sleep. I got out of bed to do my normal routine of reading my Bible while pouring some breakfast down my tube. About ten minutes into the process, my feeding tube malfunctioned. I've had it get clogged before—dozens of times—but with a gentle shove of the syringe plunger, we're flowing again. Today, however, nothing would budge. I pushed as hard as I could to no avail. I stood up and placed all my weight against the syringe plunger and the wall. Nothing. Joanna came to my aid and pushed as hard as she could. Only the smallest amount went through. My feeding tube—my lifeline—was inoperable. It didn't appear to be clogged. It appeared to be broken.

This dilemma led us to pray at a heightened level. I decided to not go to a hospital immediately, but instead give the tube a few hours and see if something would change. I sent out a text message to a couple people and explained that if God didn't heal my swallow or open my tube that I'd have to go to an emergency room.

I reminded God that when I had this second tube inserted, I had prayed that this would be the last one I would have to have. Joanna and I repeatedly called out to Him—literally crying—for His touch. I decided to try a tiny bite of yogurt. Then another. We continued to pray. A half-hour later I showed Joanna the yogurt container. I had eaten an ounce. "You haven't spit?" Joanna asked.

"Nope."

I had no clear feeling of swallowing, but for the first time I had no demanding need to spit. Slowly, I kept testing the yogurt. At the two-ounce point, we started to really get excited. Our prayers went to a higher level of praise, declaration and intercession. Then I tried a small swig of orange juice. It went down. Amazing. A tiny, tiny burp arose. Something was happening. Joanna put her hands on my neck and prayed more (something she has done dozens of times), but this time I felt a slight sensation in my throat, down by where the esophagus has been stuck for so long. As a step of faith, I threw away my spit cup. Joanna took a picture.

I began to declare it: "You have been healing me; You are healing me; You will heal me!" And then, "Greater is He that is in me than he that is in the world. Greater is He that is in me than he that seeks to destroy. Greater is He that is in me than the disease that is in me. Greater is He that is in me than anything that is against me."

Two ounces of yogurt and a swig of juice don't usually lead to great celebration, but today they did. It was the evidence we needed that God was stepping in on this day . . . the very day my tube ceased to function. All through this journey of sickness, God has shown His sovereignty through timing. Once again He did so. On the morning my tube died, my throat came to life. Amazing.

At about the three-hour point I stared at the empty yogurt container. I couldn't believe it. I hadn't spit a drop of it out. I was eating—awkwardly and incredibly slowly—but eating.

Twelve hours have now passed. My tube is still inoperable, in spite of numerous efforts to force it or open it with substances like Pepsi. I have been eating steadily—in tiny increments, sometimes with great effort and occasionally with choking—but eating. Total consumed: eight ounces of yogurt, one-third of a banana, four saltines, some orange juice, one Wendy's Vanilla Frosty and to finish it off, a half cup of chili. Not bad for a rookie, eh?

I have so many lessons to share, so much of God to reflect on, so many calories to try to consume before I can leave the feeding tube behind; but for this moment, I just want to celebrate and I want you to do so with me.

To the hostess who believed for me this week when I couldn't: Thank you! To the brother in Oklahoma who has fasted from ice cream on my behalf for the duration of this ordeal: Your commitment is complete. Have a big bowl . . . with toppings! To the parents whose children have prayed for me with unusual regularity: Throw a "Yay, Jesus" party. Don't miss this teaching/celebrating opportunity. To all of you friends, literally scattered across the globe, bring glory to God. A God-timed miracle took place today. You were part of it. Thank Him!

May 2
A PSALM OF PRAISE

Thank you for celebrating our miracle with us! Words of rejoicing have reached us from, quite literally, all over the world.

My heart desires to continue to praise God for the work He has accomplished within me in these days. I have thanked Him in private and public, but today I want to thank Him in "print." With a slice of cheesecake on my left, the Psalms on my right and a computer on my lap, I ask you to join me in giving Him glory once again. In the form of poetry sometimes used in the Old Testament where each stanza begins with a consecutive letter of the alphabet, I offer the following:

A severe mercy was granted me;
A thousand chances to crucify self were mine.

Baffling thoughts troubled me;
Buffeted beliefs confused me.

Cries from Your saints came before You;
Calls for intervention were heard by You.

Daily, we begged You for "one touch."
Determined, we persisted like Luke's widow.

Every morning we arose by Your grace;
Every night we slept in Your care.

For weeks we heard only Your silence, O Lord;
For months we searched our souls.

Gone were the quick solutions and trite theology.
Glaring in the mirror of our souls, we faced our own questions.

Help from Your throne seemed to be delayed;
Healing from Your hand seemed to be denied.

I determined to declare Your goodness in pain;
I was driven to new depths of the soul.

Journals of ancient saints gave me comfort, while
Judgment from a few current saints gave me pause.

Knowing Your Word gave me stability.
Keeping Your Word gave me hope.

Love flowed to me from Your beautiful bride;
Likenesses of You were seen in Your precious people.

Many believed for me when my faith faltered;
More heard of my cry and joined my prayer.

Never did You leave me, never did You abandon me.
Now I can see that You were always present.

Opening Your hand in Your sovereign time
Opened my throat after such a dry season.

Quiet tears stream down my face, as
Quenching water flows past my lips.

Rejoicing hearts join in our joy;
Resounding praise ascends to Your throne.

Senegal's darkness is pierced by a joy-burst;
Schoolroom questions are answered in truth.

Tears fall into Iraqi sands;
Testimony is heard behind Israel's walls.

Under the Fiji sun, joy finds companionship.
Under an Oregon rain, stories of Your kindness are told.

Very young voices give praise to their Daddy.
Via Twitter and Facebook, many echo their song.

Windows open to Black Forest shouts.
Widows rejoice as their pastor-son swallows.

Extreme gratitude is due You, O Great One.
Excited rejoicing arises to Your throne.

Yes! We will continue to celebrate Your goodness.
Yes! We will always declare Your praise.

Zeal for Your glory ascends from our grateful hearts.
Zeal for our good descends from Your generous throne.

Praise be to the Lord, the All-Wise God
Who is always with us, but ever beyond us;
Ever revealing Himself to us, but always hidden in mystery.
Praise Him, young and old.
Praise Him, near and far.
He has revealed Himself to His servant.
He has displayed His glory to His undeserving one.

Well, the last bite of cheesecake is in my mouth (praise God again!) and the last moments are left on my laptop battery. Meanwhile, my Bible will stay open and my mouth will stay full of praise . . . and food (hopefully in that order).

Talk to you again soon.

On the journey with you,
John

BABY BITES AND BIG LESSONS

May 14

It's been a little over two weeks since what one friend of mine has called "The Swallow Heard 'Round the World." My joy has been doubled by hearing of your joy. Thanks for celebrating with us. It's fun to picture the scenes you've described from Austin, Texas, to Arlington, Washington . . . from the Black Forest of Germany to the deserts of Morocco. God is being praised, and that makes me happy.

Baby Steps, Baby Bites

I wish I could say that I am freely eating anything in sight, but the fact of the matter is that those little swallow muscles had been dormant for eighteen months and I must still be careful about what I attempt to consume. At least once a meal, getting a little greedy, I take too big a bite and break into a coughing fit.

As a result, I'm still relying significantly on my feeding tube (it's working fine now). While I'm still a long way from taking on a buffet, my nibbling and sipping are gradually getting stronger.

It Doesn't Take Much

Picture this scene: I'm seated in a fast-food place with my family. Various assortments of burgers and fries fill the table. Pleasant conversation and laughter flow as freely as the iced tea. I'm eating with them, albeit only one French fry, one nibble of Joanna's sandwich, a sip of her tea and a couple bites of ice cream. A part of me wishes I could just be normal and eat freely like they do; but the fact that I can do *something*—that I can nibble and sip—makes *all* the difference. The pain of isolation is gone. The sting of feeling left out is over. I feel a part again.

Another example: A year ago I was so weak I was unable to do any household chores except pay the bills . . . in itself, a laborious task on multiple dimensions. I lived with disappointment that I had found nothing to alleviate all the extra work I had caused Joanna. Then I got an idea: I could empty the silverware basket after the dishwasher was finished. This attempt to help Joanna probably only saved her ninety seconds, but it was something I could do. I was now making a contribution—miniscule though it was—and felt encouraged by it.

I think there is something to be learned here that should be applied more broadly. Whether it is a child on a playground, a member of a church, a volunteer in an organization or a guy sitting at a fast-food table, a little involvement goes a long way. Too often people are left out entirely because their contribution is considered small. As one who has just moved from the awkward place of watching others eat, to joining them—albeit in a very small way—I testify that there is a massive difference. Finding even small ways for people to participate can bring more blessing to their lives than you would anticipate. To be included—to belong—is the longing of every heart.

Countless people will never be the "lead actor," but if they can have a "bit part," they will experience the pleasure of the whole production.

Running in the Dark

Repeatedly this past year, Joanna—my wife, friend, caregiver, counselor and coach—has talked to me about the life of Joseph. Sold by his brothers, hauled away as a slave, falsely accused and then literally forgotten in an Egyptian prison, Joseph had no way of knowing when or even if his trial would end. The dreams he once experienced now mocked him. The life he once enjoyed was now just a distant memory. Month after month he faithfully obeyed God in a forgotten state.

Had Joseph known that in just weeks or days his trial would end, it certainly would have been easier to endure. Had he known he only had one more mile to go on this grueling marathon, it would have been easier to persevere. But his trial had no mile markers. God Himself had marked off the finish line, but God alone knew where it was.

Joseph didn't have any more reason to hope the day before he got released than he had during his entire imprisonment. There was an end to his tunnel, but it was hidden by a sharp bend . . . a sudden turn of circumstances that he had no way to see.

I am impacted by the fact that Joseph stayed faithful to God during the dark days. His character was tested by trial. His faith was stretched to painful lengths. Each new day looked as bleak as the previous one.

Yet, suddenly—without warning—it was over. The trail of trial abruptly ended. Certainly there would be other lessons to be learned, but this long, grueling journey ended—never to be lived again. I love the picture that when the news of deliverance comes, Joseph is just one shave away from being ready to stand in the pharaoh's presence.

Through the year and a half of being unable to swallow, I took heart from Joanna's insights. I knew my "coach's" observations were correct. I related completely to the "tunnel blindness" of Joseph's story. On April 26, the day before my healing, my difficult situation didn't look any brighter than it had any other day. In fact, on the day of healing, my morning began without any sense of hope that this might be the day a miracle took place. Like Joseph, I had no way of seeing my deliverance coming.

But suddenly it happened. I rounded the last curve and unexpectedly found myself in daylight—blinded and confused—but out of the tunnel. I'll probably have many more "tunnel marathons" to run in life. Hopefully this will be one of my worst, but it likely won't be my last. I'll run in the dark more effectively if I am confident that God knows where the finish line is and if I leave that detail to Him.

I pray that those of you who are still running in the tunnel will find encouragement from these words today.

Your fellow traveler,
John

May 20
TEST-TAKING TIPS

"Don't be surprised by the many trials you are facing," the New Testament authors advise us.

Tests are an expected part of our journey. No one is immune. There was only one "get out of jail free" card and Adam lost it in the Garden. This you already know. But you may not have thought through some of the following. I pray that you will be encouraged by these insights into handling life's hardships.

Tips for Taking the Tests of Life

1. Every test is an open book test.

    It didn't happen very often when I was in school, but I always loved it when my teacher or professor announced that we could use our notes or textbook in taking the test. Good news: God has given us the finest resource—the Bible—and welcomes us to keep it wide open during our trials. Joanna and I have always been students of the Word, but in this era of testing, our commitment to turn to the Word every day has only increased. This has been a key to our emotional, spiritual and relational health during this hardship.

    If you are in a trial, stubbornly resist the temptation to withdraw from the Word. This *will* be a temptation for you. There were months in this journey that my Bible reading time was 100% determination and 0% inspiration. I've referred to that era of Bible reading as feeling like "sandpaper" to my soul. Yet, Joanna and I persisted and testify that we are the better for it. Keep the Book open. Feed your weary soul. Seek your Father's heart.

2.   Every test is a group project.

On a rare occasion, my teacher or professor would announce that the project or exam was going to be done in a group context. I didn't always appreciate this. I liked to work at my own pace and do my own thing. I can be a bit of a "loner." However, in the tests of life, God never intends for us to bear them completely alone. He's placed us in a spiritual family with brothers and sisters for a reason. To be sure, some of those family members will disappoint us in our time of trial; forgive them, knowing we have done the same thing to others. Resist the temptation to isolate. Determine that you won't wallow in your private pool of self-pity. Keep opening your heart to others who in a direct or indirect way will walk with you through this ordeal.

3.   Every test is a personal encounter with the Instructor Himself.

If I am able to finish my doctoral program, I will have to give an oral defense of my work. This will be a "test" unlike any I've had in my academic past. However, I look forward to it because it will be a personal encounter—a dialogue—with people I've come to respect. In a much more significant and personal way, every test we face can be a personal encounter with God the Father, Son and Spirit. Our mysterious God reveals more of Himself to us through hardship than in any other way I know. You don't have to like your personal test, but you will have less angst and more hope if you see the test as an opportunity to enter into new dialogue and deeper relationship with God.

4.   Every test elicits something deeper from within us.

In our school days, exams drew out of us knowledge that we had acquired. Often we didn't realize we had learned something until we were tested on it. Of course, the opposite was also true: We didn't know how little we knew until we were tested on it.

I want to encourage you today that in your "life-test," you are not being graded as much as you are being guided. The Guide, our kind God, wants to use the test to draw deeper things out of us . . . to carve deeper furrows into our shallow hearts so that roots of truth can reach further into our being. I think this is part of what A. B. Simpson (founder of The Christian and Missionary Alliance) was suggesting in the following:

> *Pressed out of measure and pressed to all length;*
> *Pressed so intensely it seems beyond strength;*
> *Pressed in the body and pressed in the soul,*
> *Pressed in the mind till the dark surges roll.*
> *Pressure by foes, and a pressure from friends.*
> *Pressure on pressure, till life nearly ends.*
>
> *Pressed into knowing no helper but God;*
> *Pressed into loving the staff and the rod.*
> *Pressed into liberty where nothing clings;*
> *Pressed into faith for impossible things.*
> *Pressed into living a life in the Lord,*
> *Pressed into living a Christ-life outpoured.*

Traveling with you,
John

———o∾∾o———

"I was crushed . . . so much that I despaired even of life,
but that was to make me rely not on myself,
but on the God who raises the dead."

(adapted from 2 Corinthians 1:8–9)

June 3
SADDLE UP!

I keep encountering a simple truth: We are participants in the work of God.

He could do everything for us. He certainly doesn't need us. But, in His grace, He partners with us. He lets us participate with Him.

Earlier this week, Joanna ran across a verse I hadn't noticed before that makes the point again: "The horse is made ready for the day of battle, but victory rests with the LORD" (Proverbs 21:31). We have our part to do—getting the horses ready—but He is the one who wins the battle for us.

For me in these days, the "horse preparation" includes continuing to try to coax my muscles back to health through exercise, working toward completion of my doctoral program and attempting to be proactive in many areas of life. I'm not sure what "horse preparation" you need to do. What I do know is that "waiting on God" is rarely a passive state. It usually includes some involvement on our part.

Isaiah prayed, "Yes, LORD, walking in the way of your laws, we wait for you" (26:8). In other words, "Doing what I know I'm supposed to do today, I wait for the Lord to do what only He can do."

Saddle up those horses and ride with me. The victory is His!

Your fellow traveler,
John

June 11
EXPECTATIONS

I'm writing this blog from a lobby of the beautiful Mayo Clinic facility in Scottsdale, Arizona. It's a bonus that I've been able to spend the last few days with our daughter and son-in-law, Anna and Jeff. They sure know how to host a dad.

The Mayo appears to be a happy place to work. The staff seems relaxed. They appear to actually like working together. Kindness permeates. They've built this place around caring for people. I feel valued.

All this changes when my doctor enters the room. He is a man who evidently views words as currency, and he's the embodiment of "cheap." He grew up in the Great Verbal Depression. Words are to be saved, not foolishly spent. His Rule of Operation (an unstated rule, obviously): "Never use a sentence when a single word will do."

I respect him, though. His silence makes one think he must be brilliant. Talking only delays the opportunity to think, and he has a lot to think about right now: me.

I take his cue. This preacher will join him in the silence and let him do his brain work.

When my appointment with him is over, I walk back to the scheduling desk and the receptionist cautiously asks me how it went. Evidently, Dr. Few Words has a reputation.

"I thought he was great," I said.

"He wasn't . . ." She was careful with her words. "Well, some patients just don't like him very well."

"I wasn't hoping to make a friend. I just wanted his medical help."

She breathed a sigh of relief and commended my approach.

And, I was reminded that the expectations we bring into a room—or a relationship—matter immensely. More than one perfectly beneficial experience has been ruined because it wasn't the experience I *expected* to have.

It's impossible to never have expectations. That's not the goal. But it is possible to be aware of our expectations . . . and alter them if they are messing things up.

- Don't expect the doctor to be your friend, too. Just let her or him be your medical expert.

- Don't expect that the fastest or most talented people on the team will become the team leaders as well. They may not have that gift.

- Don't expect your church to be your sole source of spiritual development. It should be a source, but not *the* source.

- Don't expect your neighbors to be "neighborly" and, for example, help you with your home project. If they do, fantastic. If not, you shouldn't be mad at them for not meeting your arbitrary expectations.

- Don't expect your spouse to meet all of your needs. He/she is your spouse, not your God.

You get the point.

You will write better chapters to your story as you understand what drives you.

Write on,
John

July 1
IT'S WEDNESDAY

It's Wednesday night.

It's my night to write to you . . . this blog community that I have come to appreciate so deeply.

I tried. I really did.

I started a follow-up to some previous themes. It actually has some potential, but it refuses to be written tonight.

I started a poem on the death of dreams. The dream of that died quickly.

I considered providing a summary of my day—the dying man I visited, the wounded heart I prayed for, the shocking news I heard, the raging envy I felt—but I can't. Each story is too raw, too fresh or too confidential to splatter over the internet.

As a pastor, I have a front row seat to the pain-filled drama of this world. As a husband and dad, I have a backstage pass or even a director's chair. And, as a man myself, I have an active role in this same drama—finding that I am one of the characters. Some days, like this one, I follow the script in disbelief. It doesn't read like I'd expect.

To change the metaphor: Like a sneaker wave at the coast, today tried to catch me unguarded and sweep me out to sea. I'm grateful for the solid footing established through the faith that has been rebuilt this past year. The wave didn't carry me away, but my sneakers are awfully soggy and I'm chilled by the splash.

Give me a little time. I'll find a towel and dry off. I'll clean the sand out of my shoes and head out again.

But for the moment, I have little to say. I process better in silence . . . at least the deepest things of the soul. Something "trivial" like a colonoscopy I can process in public (remember that blog?), but when the scope takes a tour of my innermost being, I must pause, wait . . . reflect.

When the ancient songwriter Asaph had a day (or season) like this, he waited to express himself. He first had to enter "the sanctuary of God" (Psalm 73:17, NIV 1984). There he gained a perspective on the trials of his life and questions of his soul. He knew that if he had spoken too early, it would have caused harm. In his words: "If I had said, 'I will speak thus,' I would have betrayed your children" (73:15).

So, with my friend from ancient times, I will wait to speak. I will seek God's sanctuary. To try to understand is "oppressive" (73:16), but in time the Spirit will bring His counsel to my soul.

Meanwhile, I claim Asaph's declaration as my own: "My flesh and my heart may fail, but God is the strength of my heart and my portion forever. . . . As for me, it is good to be near God. I have made the Sovereign LORD my refuge; I will tell of all your deeds" (73:26, 28).

Watch out for those waves.
Dry out those socks.
We've got more miles to travel.

Your companion in the journey,
John

July 2
On Snipers and Souls and Hard Days

I know I caused some concern by my last blog. Thanks for your love and prayers in response. I hesitated to post it because I didn't want to worry you. Yet, at the same time, I have this high level of commitment to do what I promised eighteen months ago: to give you "an honest look into a mysterious journey." Hence, a post like yesterdays. I don't think you'd want it any other way. I know I wouldn't. Pretending takes too much energy.

Today I've been thinking about Elijah. He was the character in my devotional reading (1 Kings). I'm intrigued by the way he handles solitude, deprivation, death, the king and eventually the huge showdown on Mount Carmel. Before the day is over, fire has fallen from heaven, 850 false prophets are humiliated and slain, the people of God have returned to Him in repentance and a three-year drought has come to an end. Not a bad day's work for a prophet. He even got in a good run to finish the day off right. My kind of man.

Then came a one-sentence threat from the queen who hadn't even come to his big faceoff with the false prophets. She says that before the sun sets again, she's going to make sure that he is like them . . . as in "dead." The man who took on the heavy artillery of hundreds of prophets in the presence of thousands of people gets picked off by a lone sniper in the palace. The queen doesn't actually kill him, of course.

But, she does effectively kill his spirit. He flees faster than you can say "scared rabbit." And, he's suddenly so depressed he wants God to take his life—now. His attitude is, "I'd rather die than face another day." Elijah the stouthearted becomes Elijah the no-hearted.

I didn't slip that low yesterday; don't worry. I wasn't asking God to take me home. Besides, I already know His answer to that prayer: "No. I've got a job for you to do here. You tried that dying thing already, now get on with life!" (Those weren't God's exact words, mind you, but I think I got the gist of what He has been saying on that matter.)

I can relate to the "getting picked off by the sniper" routine, though. I'm amazed at how many hard days and how much bad news and how many life-changing factors I can face with relative strength, only to have one phone call or one difficult conversation completely flatten me. I feel like I can successfully navigate a field of land mines, defend against the artillery and dodge the air strike only to have some pistol in a guy's pocket take me out.

What Elijah is about to learn is that the queen doesn't have final say. She can threaten and wield great intimidation with her threats, but his life is in the hands of Another . . . and so are yours and mine.

It would take quite a bit to get Elijah back to a good place—a few really good meals, a couple long naps, some solitude, a revelation of God's presence, some new assignments and a ministry partner (Elisha). I don't think it will take this much for me, at least not this time around, although the "really good meals" part does sound very inviting! I don't believe we're supposed to take Elijah's story and make a formula out of it, "Six Steps to Soul Recovery." The example is a good one and the principles are significant, but the fact is that God works uniquely in each of us. And, a good work He does!

God's not One to leave His troops wounded on the side of the road. In my latest battle, I haven't seen Him yet, but I know He's near.

So, take heart with me tonight, wounded soldier. Your injury isn't fatal. Your enemy is temporary. Your Redeemer and Healer is near. We may have caught the sniper's bullet, but the Lord will catch us. Of that I am certain.

Fighting alongside of you,
John

July 8
UNTANGLING–PART 1

Joanna and I feel like this summer is a season for us to "untangle."

The metaphor comes from my boyhood when I spent countless hours fishing—often on the banks of the Mississippi River. Every time I fished, it was inevitable that I would need to untangle my line. Innumerable are the ways a kid-fisherman can get his line tangled, and I found most of them. As a result, I would take a seat on the riverbank and sort out the mess I created. My fishing was delayed for a few minutes, but once I got my line untangled, I was free to cast out again. No one can fish effectively with a tangled line.

As Joanna and I take a seat on the riverbank together, we find that our lives are entangled in a half dozen ways. We're proactively working and regularly praying that in the months to come we can get our lives untangled from these things so that we will be free to cast out again.

For example, I've wanted to complete a doctoral program for fifteen years. I've been enrolled in one for five years. It's time to finish. It has become a knot in my line and I need to sort it out. I have a date set aside on my calendar for my oral defense. The end is in sight! But, like a kid on the riverbank, it's time to sit down and do what needs to be done.

Another example: While our home served us well during the years I was healthy and the kids were home, it is now another tangle in our line. It's a great home. We've loved it. Yet, this is a season to simplify our finances, yard maintenance, etc. All this to say that our home is on the market. A realtor's sign—looking so out of place—hangs by our driveway. I was surprised by the emotion I felt when I saw it . . . but it's time.

Being released from the feeding tube would be another major "untangle" experience. God continues to strengthen my swallowing. I am clearly improving. Yet, I still need the tube. "Feeding Tube Freedom Day" will be exciting! I'll keep you posted. Meanwhile, I pray and munch . . . a bowl of Honey Nut Cheerios accompanies me as I write this.

So, now you know some of what Joanna and I have been working on and praying about in recent weeks. Selling a home kicks all manner of activity into action: cleaning closets, maintenance projects and garage sales (yes, it will take more than one). Finishing a doctorate has a list of its own. But with each box sorted or final project page written, we're making incremental progress toward our untangling goal.

More on this later. I think the Lord is taking this metaphor a step further in my life, but give me another week to process it.

Meanwhile, let me throw on the "pastor hat" and remind us of the well-known instructions found in Hebrews 12: "Let us throw off everything that hinders and the sin that so easily entangles. And let us run with perseverance the race marked out for us." "Throw off"—unburden yourself—and run freely. Wise words.

Jesus had something to say about this as well, "The seed that fell among thorns stands for those who hear, but as they go on their way they are choked by life's worries, riches and pleasures, and they do not mature" (Luke 8:14).

Jesus' words make me think of some of the vines that grow here in the fertile Pacific Northwest. To the naïve, they look like they are full of "life." They are green, aggressive and abundant. Yet, in a sense, they carry "death." Left to grow around your other plants, they will choke them out and take over. You don't just prune such vines. If you care about your garden or landscape, you poison or uproot them.

So, pick your picture: untangle, unburden or uproot—fishing line, extra baggage or threatening vines. My hunch is that whatever one you choose, you can probably find some way to apply this to your life as well.

Talk to you again soon,
John

July 15
UNTANGLING–PART 2

If you read the July 8 post you know that Joanna and I are in "un-tangle" mode—something we've been working on for a month now.

Recently I was taking notes during a meeting. A few minutes into it, I wrote at the top of my paper, "Did I come back from my deathbed to do this?" I surprised myself with my own words. It was a good meeting, and I was fully engaged in the conversation. However, it was a personal "reality check" moment.

I've complained enough in the past, and you know that recovery hasn't been an easy journey for me. Death would have been unspeakably easier. But, upon coming to accept that God has more for my life, I've tried to co-operate with Him in this challenging recovery process. And, I rejoice that I'm miles down the recovery path. I'm not the healthy man I was two years ago, but I'm certainly not as sick a man as I was one year ago.

Progress is definitely being made. And, now that it is, I'm back doing more things: preaching, writing, working on the final project for the doc-toral program, participating in meetings, mentoring, etc. Yet, as I do all of this—and I'm absolutely thrilled that I can be doing these things—I'm beginning to ask this new question: *Did I come back from my deathbed for this?* Or, to state it differently: *Did God give me a second chance to live so that I would give what little time I have left to this?*

This reflection has become a great tool for me to evaluate what I'm giving myself to. In the past, I often took on countless projects merely because "somebody had to do it." There was a measure of good to this, but its inherent weakness was a lack of evaluation. I now have an evaluation tool—a pair of glasses to look through—to help decide if I'm the one to take on that project or not.

These questions—these glasses—are also becoming a helpful tool to check my emotional response. I've known through the years that I can become passionate about too many things. As I look back on my life, I'm embarrassed at all the times I spoke so fervently over issues I now consider to be insignificant. I pounded tables, raised my voice, spiked my blood pressure, filled white boards and challenged the views of teammates with great intensity on far too many issues. I wasn't selective with my passion. If I had an opinion, you were sure to know. I'm trying to change.

I'm not very good at this yet, but I'm excited about the potential that awaits me with these new glasses. When my emotions arise over a subject, I'm trying to ask myself, *Did I come back from my deathbed to fight over this issue? Is this how I want to use my remaining breaths?*

Don't be concerned; I haven't lost any passion. In fact, it has probably increased. What I'm trying to change—where I'm seeking to mature—is to be more selective in these passions . . . to raise my voice on fewer issues.

And so, this too is an "untangling." Just as I'm back on the riverbank sorting out my fishing line in practical ways such as selling our home, I'm now attempting to unravel my spirit from so many issues as well.

Untangled line and new glasses. Add to that, my improved health and the pleasure of eating food. Hmmm, life might actually become enjoyable again.

Travel light. We've got more miles to go,
John

July 25
UNTANGLING–CONCLUSION

I've been delayed in posting a blog this week because Joanna and I are having the pleasure and privilege of being with a small group of young ministry couples as they experience a renewal event in the Bitterroot Mountains of Montana. We're on a 2,000-acre ranch that is quite rustic. Think port-a-potties and dust. Think great mountain views and grazing deer. Think quiet breezes blowing through pines. Think solitude. My cell phone barely works. Internet does not. I've not seen a TV in four days. We're just a half-mile from the highway that connects us to the world and its frenetic pace, but I have no desire to get back on it today. I'm away from the buzz of life, and I'm happy.

Most of us don't get to live on 2,000-acre ranches. Most of us don't even get to visit 2,000-acre ranches. Most of us live within a block of the buzz. Some of us feel like we live in the center of it.

Being on this ranch for a few days is serving me well in my quest to untangle my line. I've withdrawn from the way most of the world operates. I've leaned in to creation.

This came at a good time. You see, from a human standpoint I've not made much progress on my untangling efforts so far this summer. In fact, in some ways life feels like it's getting more complicated, rather than less so. Occasionally on that riverbank of my childhood, my inexperienced fingers only made the tangle worse for a while. Rather than eliminating the confusion, I added a loop or twist of my own.

Here's the principle I'm thinking of today: *Life complicates*. Tangles happen. Without intentional effort and/or divine intervention, our lives become increasingly complex. Untangling is a proactive and, at times, laborious process. Simplification doesn't happen naturally. Complexity does.

I believe there are countless reasons for this. Financial debt, material possessions, interpersonal relationships, physical health and many other factors guarantee that without intentional effort to the contrary, life becomes increasingly complicated.

We must be on guard—we must take the position of a sentry for our own spirit—for life can wrap us up in a knot of worry, stress and disease. The good news announced to the Christ-follower is that "where the Spirit of the Lord is, there is freedom" (2 Corinthians 3:17). I don't know all that Paul meant by those words, but I do know that many of us aren't living with a sense of freedom.

I'm calling us today to make efforts for a greater experience of freedom. Untangling is doable. A lightness of spirit can be found. Solitude, silence, simplicity and Sabbath-keeping (i.e. hearing God's permission to spend a day renewing your soul rather than conquering your "to do" list) are powerful spiritual disciplines helping us enter in to this freedom. Forgiveness is a big one, too: Nothing tangles the line of the soul quite like the skill of hanging on to a grudge. Nothing frees it quite like the joy of letting go of the offense.

I doubt if you'll be able to find your way to a ranch for a few days. Your back deck or the county park might do just as well. Wherever it is, pursue some soul-quieting places this summer. While you're there, listen to the Spirit and see if He whispers some ways to get a tangle out of your line.

We're losing daylight. Our time to "fish" is limited. I want to get in more casts before nightfall. I've got to get this line untangled. I hope you will, too.

Hmmm, maybe it's time to ask Dad to help.

Traveling with you,
John

You: A Joyful Declaration of the Sovereignty of God

August 19

You have a plan for this world.
It is good.
It includes my life.

You have a plan for this world.
It is comprehensive.
It includes all of us.

You have a plan for this world.
It is remarkable.
It will astound us.

You have a plan for this world.
It is mysterious
It is often hidden from us.

You have a plan.
I am part of it.
I submit to You today.

You have a plan.
I may not see my part in it.
I yield to You today.

You have a plan.
My pain has a purpose.
I trust You today.

You have a plan.
It includes my future.
I wait for You today.

Your plan
stretches into eternity.
We celebrate what awaits.

Your plan
spans all of history.
We accept what has taken place.

Your plan
shatters all demonic schemes.
We declare Your victory.

Your plan
secures us in Your love.
We rest in You today.

You.
You are good.
We will be blessed forever.

You.
You are limitless.
We will explore You forever.

You.
You are bliss.
We will enjoy You forever.

You.
You are sovereign.
We will be safe forever.

Everything that has ever existed and
everything that ever will exist
has always been,
and always will be about
You.

August 26
STRENGTH ENOUGH

Most of you will recognize the name of Charles Spurgeon, pastor of the Metropolitan Tabernacle in London throughout the final half of the nineteenth century. For the last two decades of his ministry, he struggled with health issues. His story has been impactful for me this past year. Let me share just one insight from his teaching today.

It seems that Spurgeon was in the habit of delivering an "Opening-of-the-Year Message." Unknown to him, January 1, 1892, would be the last message of this type he would give. He opened his final New Year's sermon in this way: "Passing at this hour over the threshold of the new year, we look forward, and what do we see? Could we procure a telescope which would enable us to see to the end of the year, should we be wise to use it?"

Great question, Charles. If we had the power to see into the future, would we be wise to use that power?

Pastor Spurgeon answered his own question: "I think not. We know nothing of the events which lie before us of life or death to ourselves or to our friends, or of changes of position, or of sickness or health. What a mercy that these things are hidden from us!"

He proceeded to explain why it would be unwise for us to foresee our blessings ("they would lose their sweetness while we impatiently waited for them") or our troubles ("we should worry ourselves about them long before they came, and in that fretfulness we should miss the joy of our present blessings").

Spurgeon concluded the thought by saying, "Great mercy has hung up a veil between us and the future; and there let it hang."

I like Charles' advice. Let the veil do its holy work of helping us live today as unencumbered by the future as possible.

However, Charles didn't live in the era of modern medicine with our arsenal of diagnostic devices, not the least of which are CT scans. Because of issues often associated with my condition, doctors both locally and from Mayo Clinic suggested that I have some of this kind of precautionary work done. Somewhat reluctantly, I obliged.

The result: It was discovered that I have a small growth in my right lung that wasn't there eighteen months ago. Based on various factors, including the size and shape of the growth, there is a 25–30% chance that it is cancerous . . . ah, there it is, that dreaded "C" word I've avoided for the duration of my illness.

Now, trying to be a "glass half-full" kind of guy, I do the math and remind myself that there is 70–75% chance that it's not cancer. Besides, my life isn't in the hands of mathematicians, but in the Master's. And, it always seems that His math doesn't quite add up the same as ours.

Seeing with a CT scan isn't quite like Spurgeon's mythical telescope, but it does allow us to see a little further than I really wanted to see. I know that my future now holds at least one more test (next week) and possibly a whole new round of involvement with the medical community. I'm sure they are nice people. I just didn't want to go to their offices. I'll keep you posted when I learn more.

All this occurs during my summer of "untangling." While I'm making concerted efforts to simplify, my life seems to have become more complicated. More than once on the riverbank of my childhood, I actually made the tangle worse. My young fingers and untrained eye increased the complexity of the mess. So it feels this summer. I've been on this bank before.

To be fair to Spurgeon, there was more to his message. As he looked to the year to come, he did believe that there were some things he could know. Most striking was his confident assurance: "I perceive very clearly, by the eye of faith, strength for the journey provided. . . . We shall have strength enough, but none to spare; and that strength will come when it is needed, and not before."

Pastor Spurgeon didn't know what the year before him held, but he knew that God would grant him the grace for whatever was to come.

With that assurance, Spurgeon lived and—before the year was over—died well. Meanwhile, his example and testimony live on. Thank you, Charles. I want to live with the same confidence: Whatever the future holds, we shall have strength for the journey—none to spare and none too soon—but enough. That resonates with me. It matches what I've experienced in my walk with God. I'm thinking it matches yours as well.

Blessings to you this week.
Thank you for being part of this community.

On the bank, but not the brink,
John

September 2
WHEW!

Did you hear the deep sigh that came from my corner of the globe?

This morning I received a call from my doctor informing me that the latest scans results indicate that the mass on my lung is most likely scar tissue. It does not appear to be an active tumor. I am to have another scan in a few months to make sure that the mass has not grown but it appears that the issue is a nonissue. Thanks for praying with me and for your encouragement during this most recent round of medical involvement.

My Bible reading plan yesterday took me to 1 Chronicles 19. David's troops are once again involved in a battle with various opposing forces. On this particular day it feels like the enemies are coming from every direction. The commander of Israel's army has a simple battle strategy and then encourages those under him to "be strong, and let us fight bravely for our people and the cities of our God. The LORD will do what is good in his sight" (19:13).

Be strong. Fight bravely. The Lord will do what seems good to Him. These words came to me yesterday as an encouragement and a challenge. While I felt like I was being surrounded by yet more enemies, the Lord's instruction was to be strong, fight bravely and live with a deep confidence that He would accomplish His good purposes. I'm grateful today that He saw fit that one of the enemies I don't have to fight right now is cancer. Obviously this came as a great relief and gives me new focus to fight the enemies that I do have. I am encouraged to re-engage my battle with this muscle disease and my efforts to get off this feeding tube. Other enemies of the soul always try to find their way to the front lines, but the bottom line is that the Lord's good purposes are being accomplished as we take courage and fight bravely.

Thanks for standing with me. I trust that you sense I am battling alongside you in whatever enemies you face today as well.

Together for His Kingdom,
John

September 9
ABOUT FORMULAS, FAITH AND LIFE CHANGE

When I was released from ICU and it appeared that I had dodged death, I remember people saying things like, "I can't wait until you are well enough to preach again. You are going to have such profound insights from this experience." People hoped I had a glimpse of heaven, assumed I had significant encounters with God and just knew that I would have life-changing truths to share with the world. The formula was: "The worse the crisis the greater the lessons."

Maybe in time this will be true. Maybe with enough reflection I'll be able to articulate some earth-shattering principles. But meanwhile, the only thing "profound" that I feel is profoundly disappointing. If you are looking for some new life-changing power principles, I'm not going to be of much help. I didn't get a tour of heaven or a personal revelation. What I did get were mounds of medications, days of hallucinations and months of rehabilitation.

In case I sound negative, let me hasten to say that this has been a life-changing experience. I'm not the same man I was before. Frankly, I miss some of the old me; but he seems to be pretty well gone and a different character emerged out of that ICU ward. Don't get me wrong: I still recognize myself—I still have some of the same passions, interests and personality as before. But, in countless areas, I'm a different man. My wife will vouch for this as well.

I'm beginning to think that this is the greater point of going through a crisis. I'm beginning to conclude that our "great crisis = great lessons" formula is wrong. I'm concluding that *who I am becoming* is more significant than *what I am learning.*

Now, certainly, what I learn greatly impacts who I become. But when the crisis is past, the greatest issue is character development. Grab whatever lessons you can. Sharpen your theology along the way. These are important and formative. But they are the smaller pieces that make up the larger subject: you.

You cannot go through a life crisis and come out the other side unchanged. The fire will consume or refine—devour or strengthen—but it must leave its mark upon you. Adversity doesn't have to harm us, but it must alter us. And you, of course, are the only one who gets to choose whether this change will be for the better or the worse.

Options

Over the months I've faced some discouragement because my recovery is so slow and unpredictable. I'll go for a week of feeling like my pain is going away and becoming a thing of the past only to have it flare up again and become a continual reality. I'll have a day when I can swallow most anything only to be followed by a day when swallowing feels like so much work it's hardly worth the effort. I could go on with examples, but the result is that I have to enter a new round of resolve to face and fight this malady. I cannot hide. I will not quit. The journey continues another day.

I didn't choose my crisis. Perhaps it chose me or I was chosen for it, but I would have never signed up for the experience. I do, however, choose every day how I will respond to it . . . multiple times a day in fact.

Here are my options:

- I can choose the ever-nagging voice of self-pity: "Someone take mercy on me. Can't you see I'm in pain?"

- Discouragement and depression like to add their voices: "You are just a shell of who you used to be. Quit trying so hard to get better or be a better person. It's not worth it."

- And then, of course, anger tries to join the choir: "You should be mad at somebody about this. Blame someone: your doctors, God, your board, yourself."

- Meanwhile, the voice of the Spirit is singing His own song: "My grace is sufficient for you. My presence will never leave you. My purposes will be displayed in you. My character can be formed in you. My glory will be seen by you. I am good. Look for signs of My goodness around you."

Every day—multiple times a day—I choose which voice will sing the loudest in my heart. Every time I make such a decision, I am being formed into the image of that voice. The same is true for you.

Back to Math Class

I tend to resist formulas, but if I had to create one to replace the previous one I mentioned, it would look something like this:

$$Crisis + Response = Life\ Change$$

Who I am becoming is a direct product of how I respond to the crisis before me. The "crisis" can be as minute as being disconnected from a phone call or being overcharged two dollars at the store. Or, it may be as massive as hearing a doctor say that your child has only months to live. You rarely get to choose your crises. They have a way of just showing up.

What we do choose is how we will respond. I'm certainly not the first to write on the subject, and I hope I'm not the last. Hasn't someone already said, "Life is 10% what happens to you and 90% how you respond to it"?

I'm seeking to choose responses that allow my crisis to become a positive factor in making me a better person. I'm challenging you to do so as well.

So let me repeat myself as I close today. We cannot go through a life crisis and come out the other side unchanged. The fire will consume or refine—devour or strengthen—but it will leave its mark upon us. Adversity doesn't have to harm us, but it must alter us. We alone choose whether this change will be for the better or the worse.

Together with you in this journey,
John

September 16
IN THE MOMENT

One of the exceptional characteristics of Jesus—a characteristic we rarely discuss—is His unusual ability to know the future without allowing it to ruin the present. He could fully enter into the moment at hand, even though He knew what was to come.

Case in point: As you read the Gospel of Mark carefully, you discover that by the time of the Triumphal Entry Jesus has already told the disciples three times, in specific detail, about His forthcoming betrayal, persecution and death. The Father has revealed to the Son full knowledge of what awaits Him.

I can't speak for you, but knowing this was coming would mess up my day big time. Knowing that one of my friends would sell me out, that the most respected authorities of the day would pronounce me a blasphemer, that I would be seriously abused verbally and physically, that the rest of my friends would bail on me and that my battered body would be affixed to a cross—one of histories most painful and shameful ways to die—would keep me up at night and make me none too pleasant to be with during the day.

Not Jesus.

He "parties" first. I don't mean to be sacrilegious. Maybe there's a better descriptor you could suggest for me, but I'm not sure what else to call the Triumphal Entry. It's festive. It's fun. It's big. It's loud. People shout and celebrate. They rejoice and decorate. It's a spontaneous eruption of fun, joy and praise. It's an ancient equivalent of a World Series Champion's Ticker Tape Parade.

Today as I read the story I had to ask myself, *Could I enter into the party if I knew what pain awaited me? Could I rejoice before my rejection? Could I enter into the moment, knowing how fleeting it was?*

Jesus is modeling so much for us in this story. I can't capture it all. But one summary statement I can make is: "Life is made of moments. Live them."

The moment will pass. Life will move on. The sun will set again and we'll flip another page on our calendar. We can't change this.

And, pity the person who tries too hard to live the moment by attempting to cling to it. Every high school class reunion has someone in attendance who never made it out of high school emotionally. Those, sadly, were their best years, and they're still trying to live them. Maybe this isn't the clearest example, but you know what I'm talking about. Parents have tried to keep their youngest child young too long. Some athletes can't accept that their time is done and look silly playing one too many seasons. This is a fairly common issue, but it's not my main point.

I'm impressed by a Christ who is willing to throw His own party (He arranges for the colt and chooses His route and the timing of it carefully) while knowing that the party will be over so very soon. He rides into the crowd and receives their adoration. He's fully alive in the moment.

Why didn't the coming pain ruin the present moment for Him? I can't know for sure, but here are a few of my guesses:

1. Jesus knew that He would have enough grace for the pain to come. The experience would be hard—grueling, actually—but not without grace.

2. Jesus knew that pain wasn't the final word. As clearly as He saw the persecution that awaited Him, He also saw the resurrection, the glory, the climax. The chapter wouldn't end with a whip, a cross or a tomb. It ended with Him finding His way back home— a really nice one at that.

3. Jesus knew that every moment had a purpose and shouldn't be overlooked. I don't think Jesus ever had a conversation, met a person or experienced an event He didn't feel to be important. He saw significance in the people and occasions He encountered.

Those of us who have dying loved ones, graduating teens or transitional living situations have very obvious ways we can apply this lesson. For others of us, the application may be more subtle but no less important.

G.K. Chesterton once said that God is forever young and it is we that have grown old. God, with a childlike delight, looks at the sunrise or spring flower bloom and says, "Do it again. Do it again." It is we who grow bored, cynical and fearful—old in our spirit—and fail to delight in the moment.

But it doesn't have to be this way. The same Christ is willing to live out His life through us today. The same grace He received is available for us. The truth He enjoyed—that pain doesn't have the final word—is true for every one of His followers still.

Life is made of moments. Let's live them well today.

Traveling with you,
John

My Seatmate

This week I had the privilege of sharing my story with the staffs of two great ministries in Colorado Springs: Focus on the Family and the Christian and Missionary Alliance. On the flight back to Portland from Denver, I had the middle seat. It was a beautiful, sunny fall afternoon. The woman in the window seat next to me didn't seem interested in conversation. I was fine with that, my voice being worn out from the previous day's speaking and conversation. But, while we rode in silence, I had to capture what I was observing and experiencing. On my notepad, I scribbled:

Clouds play among the peaks
While she plays on her laptop.
Rugged ranges roll across the landscape like waves
While the nine of hearts is slid across her screen.

Creation lies below us silently
Its testimony bold but hushed
Glorious and enduring, vast and unconquered.
It need not boast;
It is accustomed to being ignored.

Meanwhile technology captivates.
Yet another variation of solitaire
Provides sufficient entertainment for the mind
Grown accustomed to screen-sized views.
How small we are,

Smaller than a single tree stretching across the forest floor below,
But our world has made us smaller still—
Pacified by so little while truly satisfied by nothing.

The deck shuffles again for another hand
While the ranges give way to the awaiting plains.
Farms quilt the window
While more cards checker the screen.

Be not proud—O My Heart—for seeing what others miss.
Be neither naïve to think I've never done the same:
Trivialized
Marginalized
Placated by some flashes on a screen
While the beauty of creation
Or the presence of person
Or the whisper of the Spirit
Goes unnoticed.

But wait!
She looks up,
She glances out,
She shakes her head
In silent appreciation.
She sees!

The laptop is closed;
The game disappears.
She continues to stare at the tapestry below.

"Pretty cool, isn't it?" I say.
"Yes. It is," she replies with true admiration.

The nine of hearts has died,
But a human heart has come alive
At least for the moment.

Technology will beckon once again
Its voice ubiquitous
Its popularity ever rising.
But for the moment
We both just watch and admire.
Something greater than entertainment is taking place:
Worship.

246 | YEAR TWO

Year Three

Being confident of this,
that he who began a good work in you
will carry it on to completion
until the day of Christ Jesus.

Philippians 1:6

THE SETTING

The ability to eat again brought with it many benefits, including increased weight and energy. As the third year of our experience opened, I had gained back thirty pounds of the fifty I had lost. And, I believed I was ready to re-enter the world of full-time employment.

I still carried the feeding tube, more as a precaution than a daily need. I was mostly weaned from it, but if I had a setback, I certainly didn't want to have one surgically re-inserted. My voice was barely strong enough to handle the communication expectations placed on a pastor. And, our house hadn't sold. But, in spite of all this, we knew it was time to move forward. With emotion, I resigned from my part-time role at Salem Alliance, our church home for almost nine years.

Five weeks later, our gracious church family simultaneously celebrated my 50th birthday and farewell. A few days following, we were warmly received by another loving congregation, Fox Island Alliance. I was now the interim pastor for this strategic church in transition. We weren't where we thought we would be at this point in life, but we were certainly amidst kind people. The beauty of living on Washington's stunning Puget Sound was a bonus.

Throughout the year of serving as interim, I found myself turning less and less to blog writing. Preaching every Sunday and completing the doctoral program (yes, I did finish!) drew much of my writing energy.

Yet, the distance from my original health crisis—in time and geography—began to provide a helpful vantage point. My healing was continuing, both in body and spirit . . . and with it came new perspective.

JOY FROM A PRISON CELL

Today I write for those who find themselves in a place that is less than ideal. You've suffered a setback of some type. The specifics vary, but the condition is similar: You aren't where you thought you'd be at this stage of life.

My mentor today is the Apostle Paul as he writes the New Testament epistle to the Philippians. He writes this inspiring letter from, of all places, a prison cell.

As I understand the scene, chains hang from his body but not from his spirit. His physical presence is confined but his spiritual influence is not. With a tender heart for a church he's been praying for, he dictates this powerful and joyful letter. His partner, Timothy, records it. Couriers deliver it. The church is strengthened by it. Scribes preserve it. Church fathers canonize it. Translators interpret it. You and I benefit from it.

All of us realize that whether you're reading an email, an essay like this one or the Scripture itself, it's important to hear the tone of the author. The tone of Philippians is one of grateful rejoicing. Philippians should be read with an upbeat, confident energy. A warmth of fond memories and rich relationships wraps this letter like an afghan on a cold night. Trumped-up charges, imprisonment and chains only serve as the chilly backdrop for the warm fire that burns through Paul's words.

As I read the letter, I look for clues as to why Paul could be so "alive" in a place so "dead." How can his spirit stay above his circumstances? How does one authentically write an upbeat letter from a prison cell?

It's no secret why I would be on a search for such clues: I need encouragement—new winds of courage—to face my daily challenges. And, I care about others whose daily pain (emotional and/or physical) surpasses my own. Some of you are reading these words right now. And, so I search Paul's message for insight. Gratefully, I find the clues I'm looking for in the opening chapter.

How could Paul thrive in a painful place?

He sensed that his trial had a positive purpose. (Read 1:12–18.)

He sees that something good is coming out of his crisis. "What has happened to me *has served*," he testifies. There is good arising from this negative situation. The event of his imprisonment isn't an end in itself but a springboard for greater good. One example of good that Paul witnessed was that "the brothers . . . speak the word of God more courageously."

I'll confess that throughout the first year of my ordeal, as people tried to tell me this very thing about my illness, I wasn't encouraged by it. I hated my suffering so badly I could hardly care what good was coming out of it—I just wanted to be done with it. Only now am I beginning to feel some of the encouragement that arises from this truth.

For those who have eyes to see and a heart to receive, one key to being "alive" in a "dead" place is a rich awareness that our trial has purpose. Good fruit grows out of this dark soil.

Paul was convinced that his trial had an end and that the end would be good. (Read 1:19–24.)

Paul was confident that "what has happened to me will turn out for my deliverance." He knew he wouldn't be in this condition forever.

As you read carefully, you discover that Paul knew that one possible method of "deliverance" was death. He knew that a real scenario was that he wouldn't get out of that prison alive . . . and he was perfectly okay with that fact. Actually, it seems to have been his preferable choice. Dead or alive, he knew he would be delivered.

This may feel like odd encouragement, but it is helpful to be reminded that we won't always be in the situation we are in today. It does have an end point.

Paul sensed that his life still had purpose. (Read 1:25–26.)

Paul knew that he still had ministry to do with people he loved. He knew his life mattered. He believed that his life and presence would enhance the joy of the Philippian church. This is a rare perspective for someone in prison . . . in any type of "prison." Our life tends to be defined by our crisis, and our personal pain preoccupies our thoughts.

Every person needs to know that their life matters to other people. Those in pain have extra need for this assurance.

Paul believed that suffering was the norm, not the exception. (Read 1:27–30.)

I won't get invited to speak at certain American Christian conferences with this kind of teaching, but I would argue that an authentic Christian life *must* lead to suffering. For example, authentic Christianity compels us to love people we would otherwise write off. We stay invested in the lives of people who disappoint, hurt or even betray us. We show up when it would be far easier to stay away. This hurts! But it is a godly, looks-a-lot-like-Jesus-on-the-cross kind of hurt. This is just one example of many we could think of.

I believe Paul faced suffering from a healthy place because he wasn't surprised by it.

Ultimately, Paul believed that all of this—his suffering, his ministry, his life—was "for Christ."

Over and over, throughout this chapter and all of Paul's writings, there is this continuous theme: Paul's life was bound up in Christ.

I confess that pain has a way of making me even more self-centered than I already am. I want the world to revolve around me and my comfort. Paul's life reminds me of whose I am and who I am to live for.

Paul was able to write a letter of joy from a dark place. I make no claim to be living these principles consistently, but I place them before us as a model.

Grace and peace to you as you walk above your circumstances today.

John Stumbo

$\mathcal{N}\!ovember\ 18$
PACKIN' ONE LESS THING

(Body-Talk Warning: For those who are a little squeamish about things that happen in hospital rooms, you may want to skip today's post.)

I received an early birthday present today. It wasn't something someone gave me. It was something someone took away. A guy should be grateful for whatever tools and resources are used to spare and sustain his life, but that doesn't mean he can't be glad to see them go.

In the midst of a very full week of good-byes, closure, packing, celebrations, sermon preparation and generally trying to wrap things up in my final days at the church, I slipped over to the local hospital and walked out minutes later "feeding-tube-less."

Yep, the tube is gone—history, bye-bye, outta here!

I was never so happy to go the hospital. I hurried in, camera in hand. I was downright happy. Okay, I'll admit it, I was close to giddy. I know that some of you are having a hard time putting my name and " giddy" in the same sentence. I'm not normally found skipping along the sidewalk offering chocolates to everyone in sight. Yes, I brought chocolates to celebrate. This confused the nursing staff. They aren't accustomed to seeing patients bounding into their wing, greeting them loudly, grinning for ear to ear and bearing chocolate.

After all, this is the endoscopy wing. Read: Colonoscopies. Read: People trudging in having already "inputted and outputted" five gallons of toxic liquid and absolutely dreading the next hour of their lives. This is the kind of patients they normally see.

Oh, and I had a video camera, too. Usually they are the ones taking pictures—if you know what I mean. Endoscopy basically means *look inside your body cavity*. Today it was my turn to take the pictures.

Unfortunately I'm not a good multitasker—at least when it comes to removing a tube and being videographer at the same time. I didn't capture the event very well on video. Oh, well. It's permanently etched in my memory.

"Did he just say that he removed his own tube?" you ask.

Correct. That's what I said. That's what I did. Why would I give someone else the pleasure of tube removal when I was right there, too? I don't share well, I guess. I hogged all the fun to myself.

Now to those who are truly confused about all this, may I quickly explain that there are two types of tube systems. One system is held in your stomach by a "button." It is a major ordeal to implant this into your gullet and is no party to have removed.

The good news is that the replacement system—the "balloon"—is much more user-friendly. The balloon is only slightly bigger than the tube and slips into the stomach hole quite nicely. It is then inflated with water. The removal is just the reverse. Withdraw the water by means of syringe and the tube deflates and pulls out quite easily. It actually doesn't even hurt. It feels *very weird,* mind you. It's not every day you pull something out from the inside of your body . . . at least I hope this isn't an everyday occurrence for you.

Under the careful watch of my attending nurse, with right hand I held the camera and with left hand I pulled—ever so cautiously—on the tube. Time stood still. The world moved in slow motion. Trying to keep my hand steady, I pulled. Millimeter at a time it came out, gradually, ever so slowly . . . when all of a sudden, WHOOP, there it was. That nasty little mushroom-like substance (the balloon) that had resided inside my stomach for way too long was now dangling in front of me. Hideous. Ugly. Alien. Gone. The nurse quickly grabbed my traveling companion, took it to the garbage can and threw it away.

What resulted next, and has continued throughout the day, was (I hope) a once-in-a-lifetime experience. I barted. I furped. You choose which word you like best. When your stomach builds gas and finds a faster outlet than your typical options, it comes out like a wee little blow spout on a whale. It wasn't a burp because it didn't come from my mouth, but what was it? I think "furp" is my favorite.

Anyway, the nurse placed gauze over the hole, taped it down and told me my stomach would start healing over within eight hours. This is great news other than that furping will evidently only be a one-day experience.

So, for the first time in almost two years, I have nothing attached to my body. No tubes, machines, monitors, PICC lines, IVs, wound vacuums or anything! I'm attachment-free.

Such good news calls for celebration, don't you think?

"How does one celebrate such an occasion?" you might ask.

My answer: Give someone a big hug. I've not given my wife a full hug in two years . . . until today. Hugs around for everyone!

Thanks for grieving with me, supporting me and praying with me on this long journey. Today I hope you will celebrate with me, even if hugging isn't your thing. Breathe one more prayer of thanks to Jesus and add your voice to the glory-making of our great God.

November 25
THINGS UNDERTHANKED

Sometimes you just have to make up words. After all, isn't the world a little more communicative now that I've coined the word "furped"? I understand it's not a word you'll get to use every day—my little blow spout has completely healed, by the way—but if you ever do get to use it, you'll feel like you had just the right word for the right moment . . . even if it isn't in the dictionary.

This Thanksgiving morning, I'm thinking about some of the "underthanked" things in this world. The word keeps getting tagged by the spell-checker on my laptop, but I like it anyway. You see, it seems to me that God gets blamed for a lot of things and thanked for quite a few as well, but there are some things we seem to overlook on our thanksgiving list.

By the way, if any of your families do the "go around the table and tell us something you are thankful for" Thanksgiving exercise, I'm about to help you out big time.

So, here's my Top 10 Underthanked Thanksgiving List:

1. The pleasure of giving hugs. When was the last time you thanked God for the ability to hug? Not everyone is huggable and not every moment is a hug moment, but the older I get the more hugs I give. I hope this trajectory continues.

2. The ability to swallow. Dozens of muscles and nerves have to work in synchronization for us to get food or liquid from our

---

THINGS UNDERTHANKED | **257**

mouth to our stomach. Most of us do it so effortlessly that we've never thanked God for it. Join me in thanking Him for the ability as you enjoy your Thanksgiving meal today. This is the first Thanksgiving in three years that I've been able to do so.

3. A spouse or friend who can effectively tease in love. Take Joanna, for example. Today I was greeted with a warm, "Good morning, Turkey. It's your special day!" Nice.

4. One word: Cheesecake. Need I say more?

5. Getting out of bed in the morning. To have the ability and reason to get out of bed each day is something for which to be grateful. Not everyone has one or either of these.

6. Change. Many of us hate change. I'm not talking about the coins in your purse, but the continuously shifting sands of life. We think we'd like to hold on to life just the way it is. We resent good-byes, fear new situations and resist having our routines upset. As hard as it can be, change is on my list of things for which I am grateful. It's a tool that the unchanging God uses in our lives. It makes us appreciate His unalterable character all the more. It always calls more faith out of us—and this is always a good thing.

7. Death. Think me strange for including this on my list. That's okay. And, I don't want to be insensitive to the fact that often death seems to come with great cruelty at the most unexpected time. However, stepping back from the personal tragedies and taking a bigger-picture view, I must say that death is a mercy. I, for one, would not want to live indefinitely in this world in its present condition. Death must not be aided—we must do nothing to speed its coming—but when it comes, it comes with a measure of mercy.

8. Scars. My body now carries four good scars—two from muscle biopsies, one from the tracheotomy and the feeding tube hole. This last one gives me the appearance of having two belly buttons. (One more piece of information you may not have wanted to know. However, I actually think this might be very cool someday when I am a grandfather of a seven-year-old boy.) Anyway, my point is simply that each scar a) has a story and b) is a testimony that healing happens. The scar, in and of itself, isn't pretty,

but the story of healing has its unique beauty. Every person who has come out the other side of an addiction or a broken relationship can testify that although scars remain, they have a story to tell. Scars speak of hope. Five scars on Christ's body will eternally testify that salvation is real. I'm not happy that the scars were necessary, but this Thanksgiving I'm grateful for them.

9. Laughing in the dark. I remember feeling great guilt when I laughed in the funeral home where the body of my father rested in just the next room. The mortician—a friend and very funny guy—said something that cracked me up. I felt it inappropriate at the time. I don't anymore. Denial of pain is inappropriate and making light of pain is cruel, but finding reasons to laugh in the midst of pain is healing. Joanna and I have laughed and cried our way through these last two years.

10. Having Someone to thank. An agnostic friend of mine came up to me after I preached this weekend—his coming to church was a parting gift to me—and said, "The problem with believing as I do is that in a moment like this I have no one to thank but you." I responded, "And in your heart you know there is something not quite right about that." This Thanksgiving—you who have faith in the Almighty God—be thankful that you have Someone to thank for all these things and countless more besides. How sad to go through life having no one to thank beyond the human level.

Talk to you again soon,
John

December 3
MILK IN THE FRIDGE AND FEET ON THE GROUND

Dear Friends,

We have safely made the move to Washington to begin as interim pastor at Fox Island Alliance. We've already met some wonderful people, got our boxes unpacked and bought our first gallon of milk . . . not that a gallon of milk is a big deal, but it does seem a little symbolic that you're going to stay somewhere for a little while at least.

Speaking of staying, our interim role has me thinking about Jeremiah 29. The context of this chapter is that many of God's people are far from home in exile. The wise prophet writes them a letter. He's not the only voice speaking into their lives. They have many other influencers giving them a united message: "Don't unpack. You're coming home soon. No use letting any roots go down; you won't be there long enough for it to matter."

Jeremiah, as he was often called upon to do, gives them a message to the contrary. Counter to popular opinion, he counsels these exiles to do some extraordinary things . . . such as unpack. Settle in. Don't live like transients but find a routine. Forge ahead. Make decisions about your future. Don't retreat or coast. And, while you're there, be a blessing.

Jeremiah warns us of the temptation many of us have felt: "We're not going to be here very long, so what do we care about these people or this city?" Jeremiah calls them (and us) to take a completely different approach and seek the welfare of the city. Pray for its blessing. Do your part to make it a place where shalom dwells.

I see Jeremiah's advice as a powerful life principle: Wherever you are, be all there . . . even if you don't think you're going to be there very long.

This advice is significant for people like you and me who live much of our lives in checkout lines, in traffic jams or in waiting rooms of some kind. How many of us have wasted months of our lives with the attitude of "when this season is over, then I'll _____"? Meanwhile a lot of life passes us and we've only been half-engaged.

I'm aware that having "interim" attached to my title might cause some people to not want to lean into relationship. I'm also very aware that I'll be tempted to do the same. Instead, I'm seeking to intentionally counter this and be all here while I'm here.

The bookshelves beside me look like I've been here a decade. I just spent some time praying through the church auditorium like I've done in all the churches I've pastored. I'm trying to learn names and understand issues and value histories and do all the things I've tried to do in places I intended to stay much longer. I'll give this few-month run every bit of energy I can wisely give.

After all, having come so close to death, I no longer take for granted that I'll have a long lifetime to preach, or write or love. Any sermon could be my last, so there's no time to be half-hearted.

All this to say, I'm all in. Here. Now. In this place for this season.

And, I'm challenging you to be the same wherever you reside today . . . even if you think it's only going to be for a short time. Enter and bless. Lean in and love. Be there . . . all there.

Maybe it's even time to buy some milk.

Traveling together,
John

December 23
BEHIND THE SCENES OF THE FIRST CHRISTMAS ... AND THIS ONE, TOO

I don't know all that took place in heaven, but I do know they talked.

I don't know all that was said, but I think He boasted.

I don't know all that He saw in her, but I do think we have a few clues.

Here's the story as I understand it: The Eternal Father declared that the fullness of time had come for the Word to become flesh and live among men. He would be named *Jesus—Yahweh saves*. He would be born as a child. He would come to the world He made, although the world would neither recognize nor receive Him. The Father went on to explain His plan to the angels and appointed one in particular, Gabriel, to carry the message . . . first to Zechariah and then to Mary.

I imagine that to the angels, Zechariah, a priest, seemed likely enough to be a candidate to be part of the original Christmas story; but the selection of Mary, a peasant girl, might have turned a few angelic heads.

As I imagine the story, it is at this point that God begins to boast about His girl:

"Mary. Ah, have you noticed the young Mary of Nazareth? She's such a trusting child. So sweet, so accepting, so open to the world I created and the word I speak."

The angels lean in to listen closer. They like it when the Creator gets in these "fatherly moods." With a smile as wide as the Milky Way, He continues.

"She talks to me, you know. I love it when she does that. So innocent, so pure. Yet, she's curious, too. I like that. She always wants to know more, to understand more fully."

And on the Father goes, boasting in His daughter . . . the one He has personally chosen to be the mother of His Son.

You may think I'm totally making this up, and I'll confess to a degree I am. But I do have a tiny shred of evidence. You see, when Gabriel arrives and delivers his message to Mary, twice he tells her that she is "favored" (Luke 1:28 and 30).

How does Gabriel know this to be Mary's status? The answer, I believe, is that he's heard the Father talk. Gabriel has seen the look in the Father's eye. Gabriel can tell Mary of her favored status because Gabriel has been in God's presence and knows the Father's heart.

Have you ever thought about this? Our God is a Father who brags about His kids! We have similar scenes to this in Job 1 and Zechariah 3. He knows us, watches us and speaks of us.

My favorite moment of this nature is when the Father's heart is so full of pride for His Son that at His baptism, the Father's breaks all of His normal restraints, rips open the curtain of heaven, leans into earth and shouts: "That's My Son! That's My Boy! I'm proud of Him!"

As God chooses Mary for this holy task, He sees that she could be trusted with His Son. As He scanned the planet, He had to choose one woman to have the honor of bearing His child. She would bear, birth and be vigilant in raising Him. She would worry about Him as so many mothers do their sons when they leave home. She would grieve like no other at the cross and rejoice like no other at the resurrection. She would walk the whole journey with her Son. The Father knew she could be trusted with Him.

The Father also knew she could be trusted with sorrow.

It was not an easy thing that the Father asked Mary to do. He would warn her that a "sword would pierce her soul" (Luke 2:35). He would offer her whatever aid and hope was appropriate in the process. But as the journey developed, it would lead the young saint through ridicule, scorn, childbirth, threat, fleeing as a fugitive, raising a mystifying child and then rarely understanding Him as an adult. No, it wasn't easy being Mary.

Somehow, as American Christians, we are prone to equate God's favor with ease, comfort or simplicity. Such was not the case for Christmas' Favored One—Mary. Her journey would not be easy. Had it been, she may not have reached the level of honor she is due.

Oh, I know, some forms of Christianity seem insistent on taking her story too far by elevating her role too high. Some renditions of the faith seem to make her a female deity to be worshiped. This isn't the gospel. This isn't New Testament Christianity.

But let's not over-react. Let's appreciate the role she played and the woman she was. More than that, let's celebrate a God who chooses to use simple people—like a peasant girl—in His greatest story. And above all, let's consider the concept that He's a Father who likes to brag on His kids.

Are you His child? You may not have the status or reputation of Mary . . . but then again, maybe you do in His eyes. His eyes continue to roam this earth looking to encourage those whose hearts are fully yielded to Him (2 Chronicles 16:9). He's the kind of Father who takes pride in His kids. Yep, that means you, too.

So, to all my friends who carry some sorrow this Christmas—to all my friends who quietly suffer in some way this season—I declare to you that your hardship may not be a sign of His displeasure. In fact, the very opposite might be true.

He trusts you. He's entrusted something significant to you. And, it just might be that this Christmas, He's bragging to a couple of angels about you.

"See her? She's staying faithful to me when the world around her is crumbling. See that guy? He's celebrating Me like he never has before, even though this is the hardest Christmas he's had yet."

I don't know much about what takes place in heaven. But, I do know they talk. And, it just might be that they're talking about you.

Merry Christmas,
John

January 6
THE PATH OF HEALING: ANCIENT LESSONS FROM THE DISEASED

His name was Naaman. He was an unlikely candidate to become an example for us.

First, he was a military commander for the enemy of God's people. That's not the first place we'd expect to find God at work. Second, he lived a really long time ago—pushing 3,000 years. We tend to look to more current examples when it comes to the subject of health. But, some of life's best lessons arise from the most unexpected places.

I've known Naaman's story since my Sunday school days. Yet as I read his story again—now through the eyes of someone living with physical difficulties—I find his example extremely relevant and timeless. I pray the lessons from his story will encourage you, especially those who battle long-term illness or infirmity.

Naaman's story is recorded for us in 2 Kings 5. We know little about him other than that he has leprosy and his army has been making raids on Israel.

In their raids, they have taken captives. He has taken one into his home. She's an unnamed slave girl. She's lost her country but not her faith. She's a slave in body, but seems free in spirit. Rather than becoming bitter about her state, she has concern for her conqueror. She testifies that in her country, prophets are able to heal.

Like those of us who are ill today, Naaman was willing to go to desperate measures to find healing. Israel was the enemy. It was his job to lead others as they beat up on the enemy. They enjoyed beating up on the enemy. But in his desperation, he goes to his enemy for help . . . something he never would have otherwise done.

Naaman wouldn't be the last to have an infirmity open new possibilities for him. How many people, who have run from God for a lifetime, turn to Him in a time of crisis? The "enemy" suddenly becomes our only hope. Such is the power of disease and hardship.

Let me simply summarize in this way:

Lesson #1: *Illness can open us up to new possibilities.*

Our infirmity can take us to places, people and principles we previously avoided or didn't even know existed. Oddly, in so doing, illness can become one of the best friends we ever had.

With a letter from the king and a caravan of provisions, Naaman begins his journey. He does what people in power typically do—he goes straight to the top, to the king of Israel. His slave girl had told him to go to the prophet, and evidently Naaman assumed that prophets reported to political rulers. He didn't understand that the prophets were under a higher authority—the King of Kings. Suffice it to say, Israel's king is not pleased to have an enemy commander requesting supernatural healing and views it as another attempt to pick a fight between the countries. Naaman's attempts to find healing are temporarily derailed. For those of us who have sought healing, this comes as no surprise.

And so arises **Lesson #2:** *The path to healing often has a detour.*

If you have gone directly from illness to recovery or from hardship to solution: congratulations. You are the minority. Most of us, even those of us who have experienced significant healing, did not experience it immediately.

As the story continues, Naaman finds himself standing outside the entrance to the home of Elisha—Israel's famed prophet. The prophet doesn't come out to greet him, but merely sends a message instructing him to wash in the river. This does not make the commander happy. This does not fit his expectations. He had a mental picture of how this was all going to play out. *The prophet is going to come out personally, wave his hand over my disease and cure me.* But his plan and the prophet's were quite different.

For those of us who have sought healing, this, too, comes as no surprise. It is **Lesson #3**: *The path of healing may not fit our expectations.*

How many times have you and I as Christians had a plan for God? We're pretty confident that we know what He should do and how He should do it. Eventually, we discover that He, whose ways are higher than ours, rarely follows our plans. He has His own for us.

Naaman is ready to abandon the entire mission. The path of healing has come to a dead end for him. He's done. The storyline reads, "He turned and went away in a rage." At that moment another voice enters the story. A servant meekly approaches him with a different way of looking at the situation.

The ill, the broken, the bruised and beaten benefit from caring outside voices. This is **Lesson #4**: *The path of healing is often preserved by a voice of reason.*

Those of us who are struggling with issues like long-term illness can sometimes lose perspective. We may not have the best judgment. Our long-term trial can erode our faith to the point that sound thinking is difficult for us. We are rescued from ourselves when we are wise enough to stay open to the wise voices around us.

Eventually, Naaman heads to the river, follows the prophet's instructions and there he is healed. Not all rivers are created equal. Naaman views the rivers of his native land as superior to those of Israel. He may well have been right. But in the process, Naaman is modeling another lesson for us.

Lesson #5: *The path of healing often leads to a place of humbling.*

It is humbling to call for the elders of the church to anoint us with oil and pray for us. It is humbling to follow the command of James 5 to confess our sins to each other. It is humbling to admit our need, our brokenness, our inability to fix ourselves. It is humbling to admit we need a Savior. Yet, healing rarely comes without a humbling. Salvation never comes without a humbling.

The healing story closes with Naaman returning to thank the prophet and declare his allegiance to the one true God. His heart has been moved and his mind convinced: "There is no God in all the earth except in Israel." In doing so, Naaman gives us the final lesson.

Lesson #6: *Healing is often more than physical. It can lead us to a new relationship with God.*

Many of us who have battled long-term infirmities can testify that a new relationship with God waits on the other end. Sometimes this new relationship is delayed by a long, dark season of an apparent absence of God. But when we come through, a deeper experience is found.

Naaman would have never chosen leprosy. Yet, his greatest problem led him to his finest moments. Actually, it led him even further; it led him to God. I don't know that any of us would choose to suffer as we have. Yet, like Naaman, great lessons—life-changing experiences—can be realized along the way.

Blessings to you in this new year,
John

February 2
LARGER SOULS–PART 1

I've been asked a few times now by blog readers if I would write about "grieving well."

The request comes from a quote that I shared some time ago. A friend of mine in Nebraska says, "Grieving well enlarges the soul."

I don't claim to be an expert on this subject, as in someone who has studied the subject thoroughly and has scientific/psychological/serious data behind what I have to say. I'm no expert, but I am a veteran. And, if you aren't a veteran yet yourself, you will be eventually as well.

Here's life as I see it:

None of us gets too many trips around this planet without loss. We lose people, friends, health, jobs, homes, money, opportunities, youth, hobbies, strength, memory, respect—and a therapy office full of other things. I spent an hour or more a day, five days a week for over a decade, keeping my body in excellent physical condition . . . to have it completely devastated in a few weeks' time. Others have built their lives with credibility, only to have their reputation demolished over one foolish decision or false accusation. A lifetime of careful savings can be wiped out—or at least seriously damaged—by one investment. We had an opportunity—it was ours for the taking—but we let it pass and it doesn't look like it will ever come again. The family member we were just beginning to value with deepest appreciation is suddenly taken from us by a tragedy. These kinds of stories have filled my office—and my journal—more times than I care to remember.

These are all losses of things we once had. Equally as painful—or perhaps even more so—is the "loss" of what we never had. We always thought we'd be married and have children. As another year passes, it's looking quite sure that will never happen. We always thought we'd get the break, the promotion. We believed that someone above us would recognize all that we have to offer, but years pass and others much younger than us climb the ladder we can't seem to even get on. The specifics vary, but I've watched it happen over and over—good people living with disappointment.

Loss. It shows up in a wide variety of forms, but none of us gets through life without it.

Grief is the human response to loss. It is right, legitimate and healthy that we grieve. To do any less is to be dishonest with ourselves. To grieve is to be human.

Then my friend comes along and tells me that my soul will be enlarged if I grieve well. This implies that grief is a skill . . . or at least something I can do poorly or well.

Again, no expert claims here, but I do think I can recognize some signs of grieving poorly. Let me start a list.

1.   *I grieve poorly when I try to convince myself that I'm not really in pain.*

We were told, "Big boys don't cry" and "No pain, no gain" and lots of other "words of wisdom" that subtly taught us to suck it up and pretend it didn't hurt in the first place. I think I know why teachers, parents, coaches and countless other adults have said these kinds of things through the decades. We actually had a good reason for it. We tell kids these things because kids don't know that their pain will go away. A kid falls and bumps his knee. It hurts like crazy at the moment of impact. He has no way of knowing that in just two minutes he's going to only have the slightest limp and in five minutes he'll have completely forgotten that it ever happened. He doesn't know this, but we—the all-wise adult—do know it, so we falsely tell him it's no big deal. At that very second it is a *very* big deal. Denying that the pain exists doesn't help us. It didn't then. It doesn't now.

2.   *I grieve poorly when grief gives way to fear.*

It is common to believe the lie that grief will never go away. Something in us says, *I don't want to always feel this way, so I won't let myself feel this way now.* Have you noticed that the most common metaphor people use for grief is "waves"? There is good reason for this because the emotions of grief do feel like they wash over us and saturate us when they come. However, some of us flee from these waves, falsely believing they will drown us. It is possible for us to accept grief while resisting fear.

3. I grieve poorly when I try to set a timeline for it.

I've thought it and likely so have you: *Shouldn't I be over this by now?* Many of us who have struggled with grief have also struggled with guilt.

In Genesis 50 we're told that when Joseph's father, Jacob, died they mourned for him for seventy days, and *then* they had the funeral, which required a very long trip. And then they had seven *more* days of public sorrow. In our American culture, people die, are honored with a service (sometimes) and are cremated or buried in five days or less. We'll send cards for a week or two after, but then if you refer to it much more the attitude feels like, *Haven't you gotten over it yet?* Grief shouldn't have a timeline and, if for some reason it does, it should be a long one. It's been often said before, "Grief is not a speed sport." The goal isn't to "get in and get out" as quickly as you can.

No doubt you can add more to this list. I'll be back in a few days with the positive side: What are evidences that I am grieving well?

Until then, peace to you,
John

February 7
LARGER SOULS–PART 2

It has been said, "Grieving well enlarges the soul."

Last week we began to discuss this idea by looking at signs of grieving poorly. Today let's look at some factors of a healthy grief process. What would "grieving well" look like?

1. *I grieve well when I believe that grief is a necessary and healthy response to pain.*

Doesn't the New Testament model this well for us? Mary, Martha and Jesus grieve unashamedly at the loss of Lazarus. Jesus pre-grieves His crucifixion. Paul grieves the condition of some of the churches. I wouldn't wish any pain or loss on you, but I would hope that when these come you'd accept that grief is a healthy response.

I just re-read the above paragraph and I admit that this sounds simplistic, but please don't miss the point: We have *permission* to grieve. Properly handled, grief is not a weak, unspiritual or unwise response. Strong people grieve. Godly people grieve. Let your heart hear the permission. You hurt. It's okay to feel it.

I first heard this permission from Joanna. When I was released after eleven weeks of hospitalization, I had hope that my trajectory of healing would be a steady course. However, when month after month passed with only incremental improvement, I had to face the reality of my loss. On more than one occasion, as Joanna drove me to yet another doctor's appointment, I would look out the van window only to see someone eating or jogging. She would survey the situation quickly and say, "It's okay. Go ahead and grieve." Simple words, but permission was granted. Tears flowed and a kind of healing began that I hadn't even thought about. While I eagerly anticipated a healing of my body, God used that season to work on a healing of my soul.

Permission granted. But to grieve well, we need more. This leads me to a second indicator of healthy grief.

2. I grieve well when I refuse to slip into self-pity.

Grief is slippery ground. It's easy to lose our footing. One moment I'm walking along honestly experiencing the sadness of my loss and without realizing it I soon slide into a muddy pit. Sadly the mud can feel good—even soothing—to wallow in. Yet, we know it's not where we belong. We need to get back on the trail and quit replaying all the "poor me" messages in our head.

I don't know if I can give you a good definition of self-pity, but my hunch is we all know when we've slipped into it. One indication of self-pity is that I really want—or even demand—sympathy from others. *Can't they see how much I'm hurting? What's wrong with all those people!* Healthy grief senses the slippery slope and doesn't let the heart linger there.

3. I grieve well when I look for the long-term good that will come to my soul.

One mental picture I have of grief is that it is a deep plow cutting new furrows in my soul.

This is one of the most important things I can tell you about grief: I believe that when we grieve well—when we don't resist the work of the plow—it increases our capacity for joy. I can't measure these things, but it seems to me that I have laughed more freely and fully—I've laughed from a deeper place—after my crisis than I ever did before. Can pain actually increase our capacity for pleasure? From my experience I'd have to say, "Yes, grieving well does enlarge the soul's capacity." This is just one of the many benefits that can arise from the hard experience. I'm sure you can list others.

4. I grieve well when I learn to forgive along the way.

Whenever there is pain, there is a cause. Usually this cause is identifiable . . . or at least we think we know who caused it. To say it differently, there is often someone to blame when we're in pain: a spouse, friend, employer, ourselves . . . even God.

To grieve well we have to get past blaming, and the only way I know to get past blaming is to release it . . . to live with the "I'm not going to hold this against you" attitude.

February is the anniversary of my father's death. Reckless teenagers killed him in a head-on collision. I can live the rest of my years angry at them or I can forgive them, letting go of my emotion toward them by accepting the fact that I did a lot of crazy things through the years too and could well have killed someone myself. When I do this (i.e. release them), my emotion is released to feel sad about the real issue: Dad's gone. He's not coming back. It hurts. Staying on task—dealing with the real issue of grief rather than forever being mad at someone—keeps my grief from degenerating into bitterness. This is big. Nothing can rot the soul like bitterness.

Hearing permission, refusing self-pity, looking for good and forgiving along the way . . . again, this is just the beginning of a list. Feel free to add to it.

It looks like I have one more "blog's worth" to say on this subject. Talk to you again soon.

Living in hope,
John

P.S. One note of caution: Please don't pass this series along to someone who has recently had a tragedy. I can just imagine a well-intentioned friend making copies of this or forwarding it to a friend who is carrying a fresh wound and it not being well-received.

The ideas I've suggested are best shared months after a crisis. During the opening days and weeks of grief, the wounds of the heart are too raw to be able to process the kind of material I've presented. If someone is fresh into grief, they rarely are helped by counsel or instruction. During the opening stages of grief, they are often more helped by acts of kindness, silence, your presence, proper hugs and touch, items of beauty, opportunities to nap, selected music, etc. There will be plenty of time for instruction. There's no need to rush to this kind of material.

So, I'd love to have you pass this along to whomever you think would benefit from it. However, I'm appealing to you to be cautious about your timing. This might be a rare instance where "later is better than sooner."

February 10
LARGER SOULS–CONCLUSION

"Grieving well enlarges the soul," my friend tells me.

In the last two blogs I've focused on the grieving aspect, but until now I've said little about the soul.

I've heard various people talk about the soul and often the conversation leaves me feeling like they've wrapped up everything about the human person they don't understand or can't identify and called it "soul." "Soul" becomes anything I can't pinch or see under a CT scan. The word becomes a catch-all for our efforts to try to describe the fact that we're more than just a body.

I'm sure that many people will disagree with this post, and I'm okay with that. If your understanding of the soul is different than mine, I'd be happy to hear it. But today I'm going to take the risk and share my understanding of the soul.

My perception arises out of teaching I received way back in Bible college days—making it neither right nor good, but a significant part of my training. I was taught that the soul is the center of our mind, will and emotions. I tabled this teaching for decades, but have come back to it in recent years as something helpful for me.

I have come to see the soul as the thinking, feeling and deciding part of me.

When I awake in the morning, I often offer to God my body, soul and spirit. I walk through them one at a time. I desire that I'd continue to experience increasing health and protection for my physical body. I want to be strong again and to run again. Next, I give Him my soul. I want my thoughts, reactions, emotions, responses and decisions to be yielded to Him. And, I yield my spirit—that mysterious part of me that communes with His Spirit, misunderstood and under-developed in many of us—to be a place He can comfortably reside.

Again, you may perceive the human being differently, and I don't mean to imply that these are distinct and separate "parts" of a human. We are mysteriously and masterfully interwoven! I freely admit that my self-understanding is very limited. To steal Paul's words: "Now I know in part; then I shall know fully, even as I am fully known" (1 Corinthians 13:12). There is Another who knows me perfectly.

But, back to our subject of grief's impact on the soul: I am convinced that a true "soul enlarging" takes place. Let me be specific from my own journey.

As I have grieved, my *mind* has been enlarged. I see things I never saw before, understand moments that once passed me unnoticed and have insights otherwise overlooked. My world is growing larger as I grieve.

As I grieve, my *emotions* are being deepened. I already spoke of this in a previous post, but I see grief as a plow doing its painful but necessary work in the soil of our hearts. Other emotions—such as joy—have increased as my soul was enlarged.

Finally, as I grieve, my *will* is being strengthened. This is perhaps the most unexpected aspect of what I'm learning.

There is an odd teaching found in Hebrews—odd for Americans, anyway. The author of Hebrews talks much about suffering throughout his work, the most startling of which for me is found in the fifth chapter: "During the days of Jesus' life on earth, he offered up prayers and petitions with fervent cries and tears to the one who could save him from death, and he was heard because of his reverent submission. Son though he was, he *learned obedience from what he suffered* and, once made perfect, he became the source of eternal salvation for all who obey him" (5:7–9, italics mine).

Suffering is a tool God has used to sanctify many of His servants; even Jesus Himself. Evidently, pain and grief are significant for our spiritual formation.

In *How Long, O Lord? Reflections on Suffering and Evil*, D. A. Carson teaches, "There is a certain kind of maturity that can be attained only through the discipline of suffering."

After quoting from Hebrews, Carson continues, "The idea is not that Jesus was disobedient before he suffered, but that in his incarnate state he too had to learn lessons of obedience, levels of obedience, that could only be attained through suffering. . . . If even Jesus 'learned obedience from what he suffered,' what ghastly misapprehension is it—or arrogance!—that assumes we should be exempt?"

I'm not claiming that I've reached some sinless state since suffering. I have all the potential to do all the hideous things my old nature craves and Satan solicits. I need Jesus and will always need Jesus to live the life He calls us to live. Nothing has changed here and nothing will. At the same time, I will testify that something has happened on the level of my will in these last few years. It feels awkward to speak of it, but I must give glory to God and affirm the words of our text—suffering became a good training school for obedience. To say it differently, while my body was being wracked with pain and attacked with disease, my will was being shaped, humbled and strengthened. It remains human and vulnerable, but some of the gaps have been filled and the rickety places solidified.

Quoting the Proverbs, the author of Hebrews goes on to challenge us, "Therefore, strengthen your feeble arms and weak knees" (12:12). I don't believe he's talking about our limbs. I think he's talking about our wills. (See Proverbs 4:20–27 and Hebrews 12:1–12.) There's nothing quite like the "weight training" of suffering to add some muscle to the bones.

So, to conclude this three-part blog, you may disagree with my understanding of the soul, but I hope you'll agree with the fundamental concept that grieving is indeed something we can do well or poorly, and when done well, we're the better for it.

And, once again Joseph's hope-filled and healing words come to mind as he declares to those who caused him great grief: "What you intended for evil, God intended for good" (Genesis 50:20, my paraphrase).

I never wanted to get good at grieving, but if I'm going to do it, I might as well do it well, knowing that God is always up to good in my life.

Thanks for continuing to walk this journey with me,
John

April 17
A PRAYER FOR HUMILITY ON PALM SUNDAY

Lord Jesus,

I can imagine that You once "rode" upon sunbeams or
*   angels' wings . . . splendid things,*
But now I see You smiling, content to ride upon a colt.

The angels praised You and heaven's elders fell before You,
But now You accept our small voices and wilting branches.

You had sent us prophet after prophet.
We ignored most of them—even killed a few.
Then You came to us Yourself;
And we did the same to You.

You don't resist. Instead, You weep.
You weep for those who misunderstand You.
You weep for us,
Even as we are in the process of rejecting You.

Who is this that mourns for His murderers?
Who is this that trades the faithful adoration of angels for the
*   fickle applause of men?*

Who is this that dismounts a rainbow to saddle a donkey?

O Humble Christ,
My angry responses to the humbling moments of my life
*   reveal that I am not like You.*

"In your relationships with one another, have the same mindset as
Christ Jesus: Who, being in very nature God, did not consider equality with
God something to be used to his own advantage; rather he made himself
nothing, by taking the very nature of a servant, being made in human like-
ness. And being found in appearance as a man, he humbled himself [even
further than he already had] and became obedient to death—even death
on a cross!" (Philippians 2:5–8, bracketed words my own).

This day reminds me again that the only way I can be like
*   You is for Your life to be lived through me.*
Until I ride heaven's winds with You, I need Your Spirit re-creating
*   Yourself within me.*

Amen.

April 19
PRAYING THROUGH PAIN

I'm thinking today about those who wake each morning with yesterday's physical pain, emotional weariness, relational loss or difficult life circumstance awaiting them.

Someone I dearly love recently said to me through tears, "Mornings are the hardest." This wouldn't be true for all of us in the midst of a trial, but I believe that many will be able to relate to the prayer that follows. The "pain" referenced could be of any kind. As humans, we have lots of places that can hurt.

He understands them all (2 Corinthians 1:3–4; Hebrews 4:14–16).

God of Comfort, Father of Compassion,

As I awoke this morning, my pain was the first thing to greet me. Instead of hearing the birds' banter or Your voice of reassurance, I hear a darker message.

My grief has not gone away in the night. As consistent as the sunrise, it awaits me.

Here's my request: I need Your help to see my trial from a vantage point higher than my own.
I want to know that my pain serves a purpose. Rescue me from the discouraging belief that my pain only works against me. Help me to

believe that by it You are producing an abundant "harvest" of beautiful things like "righteousness and peace" (Hebrews 12:11).

I want to know that my condition is temporary. Free me from the fear that this will never end. Help me believe You for miracles on this earth and for the life-giving joy that comes when I'm excited about spending eternity with You in heaven.

I want to know the unique intimacy with You that my pain can provide. Paul longed for the "fellowship" that comes from sharing in Your suffering (Philippians 3:10). May my pain cause me not to rebel against You, but to lean into relationship with You.

Without Your help, I know I don't have the right vantage point. My view is blocked. My sight blurred. But, with Your help, You can take me to lookout points to see the beauty, grandeur and mystery of Your work.

Please lift my spirit above my trial. If this happens today, I'll know that it is Your doing, not my own.

In complete dependence upon Christ,
Amen

John Stumbo

A PRAYER: ONE WEEK, TWO TREES, MANY PARALLELS

April 21

Beginning in chapter eleven of his book, Mark walks us through the story of Jesus' final week. I find it intriguing that this week begins and ends with trees—with obvious parallels and, perhaps, hidden lessons.

I attempted to harvest my reflections in a written prayer. It was my effort to further meditate on the story and honor the One about whom the story is written.

I'm not asking you to actually pray this prayer with me, although you are certainly invited to do so. However, I do hope that this will assist all of us in our attempts to meditate on our Lord during this week we call "holy."

Jesus,

Creator of All,
Lord of All Creation,
I'm fascinated to find two trees book-ending the storyline of
*   Your final week.*

The first tree You curse.
On the second, You become the curse.
At the first tree You hunger.
At the second You say, "I thirst."

To one, You speak the word of death.
On the other, You speak words of life, "Father, forgive."

The early disciples are amazed that the condemned tree dies.
I, a late disciple, am staggered that on the second tree,
    You die condemned.

I cannot fully comprehend the story.
Why would You—the All-Wise One—condemn a tree?
Why would You—the Faultless One—be condemned on a tree?

Surely You knew what was evident to many: It wasn't the
    season for a tree to bear fruit.
Surely You knew the opinion of many: There was no reason
    for a tree to bear God's Son.

The roots return to dust,
While Your soul-returned flesh ascends to heaven.

After Your work with them is completed,
The first tree never bears fruit again.
But from the second, fruit remains for all eternity.

June 9
JUNE UPDATE

"There's no easy way to do a hard thing."

This is what I reminded myself as I prepared to stand before the loving congregation at Fox Island this last Sunday. The congregation and church leadership have been nothing but gracious to us. They had invited us to drop the interim title and stay as their pastor.

In our heads, it made perfect sense to Joanna and me. But the more we prayed, the more we knew we had to say the hard word, "no."

"Yeses" are usually easy to say.
"Yes" is the feel-good answer.
"Yes" is popular.

"No" just sounds so . . . well, you know, negative.
"No" isn't fun to say.
"No" isn't fun to hear.

"Maybe" is easy to say.
"Maybe" buys some time.
"Maybe" takes no courage.

I used "maybe" as a stall tactic, but attempting to say "yes" yielded nothing but unrest in our spirits. It wasn't until I said a final "no" that peace came.

I know that not every decision can be made on whether someone is at "peace" about it or not. I know God gave us brains and expects us to use them. I know He gives us wise counsel and His Word to instruct us. I know that some people have used the "I have peace" line to defend some really bad—even sinful—choices they have made. I know there is danger in saying, "I have peace about this decision."

Yet, I also believe that we can reach a place in our spiritual journeys where we are more sensitive to the promptings of the Holy Spirit in our hearts. What made sense—what worked in our heads and gave a human sense of peace—was for us to have the stable income, health insurance, good friends and great church that Fox Island Alliance would have provided. However, for both Joanna and me, the strong undercurrent—the tug of the Spirit, we believe—was to "lean not on our own understanding" and take the route to the unknown.

So, while we're in no hurry to rush away from this great church, at some still-to-be-determined point (probably in the next few months), the Stumbos will venture out again. The uncertainty of all of this can unsettle me. At times like this I find it helpful to go back to the "what do I know" exercise. This is the mental discipline—you may even call it a spiritual discipline—of recounting what we know to be true. There is power in this practice, especially when what we *don't* know shouts loudly to us.

I rejoice to be able to say that:

- I know He will never leave us or forsake us.

- I know He has always provided for our needs and I have no reason to believe He won't now.

- I know that Joanna and I are united on the decisions we've made so far and are determined to keep standing by each other in this journey.

- I know that God uses dark corridors to lead us to good places while teaching us lessons in the dark that can't be revealed in the light.

- I know that having our faith tested is a good thing.

- I know that the God who has a plan for our lives also has a plan for this church. He will take good care of them as well.

- I know that it is my role to live today to the fullest—give my best while I am here and trust Him for what tomorrow holds.

- I know that He has brought us to a place of abundance compared to where we were two years ago (with my health, our marriage and so many other ways).

- I know that my health is better today than it was six months ago when we came here. My voice, swallow, muscles and stamina have improved.

- I know that my "did I come back from my death bed for this" viewpoint has to continue to shape our decisions.

I could probably make the list longer, but these kinds of statements provide solid footing for the path ahead.

"There's no easy way to do a hard thing." True. And this "no" was one of the hardest "no's" I've ever had to say. But in so doing, I feel like we've said "yes" to God. And, yes, that does feel good.

Traveling in the dark, with our hand in His,
John (for Joanna, too)

June 16
FINDING SOLACE IN SIMPLE TRUTHS

Tonight I'm writing a short list of the kinds of truths in which I find comfort from time to time. I write them with the fear that some people will see them as trite or toss them around like a cliché. Yet, I write them with the hope that readers who live with pain, disappointment or loss will find some solace in them as I do.

I have plenty of thoughts and ideas that run through my head in a day's time that do not promote faith, hope and love . . . or perseverance, strength and joy for that matter. They demoralize and discourage. So, once in a while I try to find some better places for my mind to go. Often those better places are found in the Scripture or a worship song. But, for tonight, I'll list a few of what I consider to be soul-stabilizing facts and admonitions.

> *Don't let the fact that you can't do what you once did keep you from doing what you can do.*
>
> *Take solace in the fact that you are a soul who inhabits a body, not a body that happens to have a soul.*
> *Your soul will live long after this body wears out and a new body that never wears out will be given to you at the resurrection.*
>
> *Quit measuring your worth by the amount of work you've accomplished, and rejoice that God sees your worth in who and Whose you are.*

Refuse to let your identity be shaped by anything that a doctor or
*   another person says to you or about you.*
Instead, find strength in the fact that your true identity is who
*   God says you are.*

Marvel in the fact that the Son of God—the King of Kings and
*   Lord of Lords,*
before whom all creation will someday bow and worship—
*   dwells in heaven*
bearing scars.

You will be tempted to quit.
This is normal.
Don't be surprised when the temptation comes.
Recognize it for what it is and walk away from it.
You didn't come this far on the journey to just give up now.

You are only given grace for today.
God doesn't give us a grace advance.
But He does give us the grace we need for the moment.

Healthy roots grow in deep soil.
Deep soil is only produced through pain.

Grace, mercy and peace to you,
John Stumbo

October 27
THE FINISH LINE FOR YEAR THREE

As many of you will remember, this journey that you've joined me on started three years ago when, during the last days of October, my health plummeted and my world changed.

Call me nostalgic, but anniversaries cause me to reflect. In today's blog, I'm trying to capture a few of my conclusions . . . to share with you some of the principles that strike me as significant now that I'm three years down this path. I pray that you will find them helpful and encouraging as well.

Looking back over this journey, I realize that:

1. *You can make it through just about anything if you have someone to go through it with you.*

I was amazingly blessed to have so many walk with me through this. No one, of course, did so more closely and faithfully than Joanna; but most of you who still read this blog in some way shared the journey. Please accept my "thank you" again. You didn't get a personal response from me for your card or email, but you blessed us along the way.

This leads me to say, don't measure the impact of your efforts to encourage by the response you receive back (or lack thereof). Some of you have the gift of encouragement. God has used you in countless lives.

However, many of those recipients (such as me) were too weak, weary or overwhelmed to respond. Like the seed-flinging farmer in Jesus' parable, keep freely sharing your words of hope and encouragement. Sometimes your words will land on "hard soil." That's okay. Imagine how sad a world it would be without those words being shared.

But back to my point, I've had some very hard stretches on this trail. It has made a world of difference to have companions along the way. It's okay that not all of these companions could empathize with my situation, as long as it was obvious that they truly cared. It may not solve the problem, but it does make a difference to know that someone cares.

2. *It is easier to accept that I can't do everything I once did, if I can still do something.*

For a long stretch of this three-year journey, I was completely cut off from some things I once enjoyed: leadership, exercise and eating to name just three examples. This was excruciating for me. To be completely stripped of activities you once enjoyed . . . and to have lost them suddenly . . . is devastating. I hated this season.

Now, a measure of everything that I once lost has been restored. I'm not doing these things at the level I once did them, but at least I get to do something and this makes a world of difference to me.

If someone can't contribute to the degree they once did, at least try to include them to the level of their capacity. The financially struggling may not be able to provide the whole meal, but give them the opportunity to provide what they can. The elderly may not catch the whole conversation, but at least be sure they know the gist of it. I couldn't lift every box we put into our moving truck, but I found the ones I could.

Don't fall prey to the "all or nothing" mentality of some. The, "If I can't do it like I once did it, then I quit" mind-set can show up in a lot of places. Resist it.

3. This leads me to a related point. I've said it before, but again I say to those of you who've experienced some measure of loss: *The fact that we can't do what we once did must not stop us from doing what we can do.*

It takes discipline, character and humility to offer what you have to give, knowing full well it's a meager offering compared to what you once gave. Yet, the "widow's mite" was a Hall of Fame Offering in Jesus' estimation.

Frankly, pride has kept countless people from bringing their final "offerings" to the Lord.

It felt good to preach when I had a strong, solid voice. Now that my voice sounds like it's been run through a paper shredder, I have to fight my pride every time I preach.

You, like me, may be embarrassed by the size or quality of your "offering," especially if you were once able to give so much more. Again, I say it: Don't let the fact that you can't do what you once did keep you from doing what you can do.

4. *We all grow old in body—some of us just get there faster than others.*

5. *We need not grow old in spirit.*

A spirit can become more "alive." The spirit is not under the same laws as the physical world is. Radiation, gravity, disease, injury and a million other elements of the physical world work against perpetual vitality in your body. However, the spirit operates in a completely different realm. "Inward renewal" is possible in the midst of "outward wasting" (see 2 Corinthians 4:16).

6. *Of all the things that change, I seem to change the slowest.*

I prayed about it again this morning. "God, how is it that I've gone through such traumatic events in recent years and yet still struggle with some of my same responses?"

I amaze myself. You'd think that a month on a deathbed, a river of pain running through my body, eighteen months of not swallowing and a few other trials would be powerful enough to revolutionize a guy, but the human nature is ancient and anchored.

My only hope for real character transformation remains the same: I need Jesus. His character arising and releasing through me are my only means of true character change.

7. *Suffering can be a powerful tool for good in our lives.*

It's easy to get lost in theological conversations at this point with questions such as, "Are you saying that God caused your crisis?" I'm not trying to approach that subject today.

Instead, three years down a path I never would have chosen, I celebrate that good has resulted. Let me name a few specifics: Joanna and I have a much stronger, happier and richer relationship; I preach, write and coach from a different "place"; other crisis-stricken people have related to my story, and God has been the recipient of some genuine glory-giving.

I'm guessing at this point someone might wonder, "Was it worth it? Would you do it again if you had the choice?"

At year three, my honest answer is "I don't know." I don't know if I would have had the will or courage to face these years, even if I had known in advance the good that would have resulted. Maybe I'll be able to answer the question better by year five.

However, I can say this: Had I known the good that would come of it, I would have had more of a sense of purpose in the midst of the worst of the storm. People tried to tell me that God was up to good kingdom work, but all I could feel were the floodwaters. Now I'm happy to say that the flood has receded enough that I can see some of the good work that resulted.

8. *God's silence does not equal His absence.*

There have been times in the last three years that I truly believe I've heard from God. I've definitely sensed His nearness. I've watched His provision unfold before me. Yet, these moments have been interspersed by days and months of silence.

Let me give two examples: For over a year we prayed for healing, yet saw very little evidence that healing was coming. God seemed silent. In recent days, I've tried to listen for God's direction on some specific decisions I need to make, yet feel no guidance.

My human response is to interpret God's silence as His absence. *What did I do wrong? Is He angry with me? Don't I have enough faith?* These kinds of questions are my mind's way of saying, "Something is wrong. I need to fix this."

But perhaps nothing is "wrong." Perhaps He has good reason for the timing of the direction He gives. Perhaps we learn lessons in the waiting room that are rarely learned anywhere else. Perhaps He's waiting for my heart to be in a place where I could actually receive what He has to say. Perhaps I'll never understand the reason for the apparent delay, but I can at least trust that, in His time, His presence will be manifest again.

I pray that there was something on that list worthy of your reflection today.

Grace and peace to you,
John Stumbo

Conclusion

THE SETTING

Almost four years have now passed since this mysterious journey began. I still battle some of the effects of my illness, but my quality of life is quite good. I haven't been able to re-enter the world of running, but I'm among the happiest eaters and preachers you'll ever meet.

Joanna and I have taken up residence in a small cottage in Wisconsin. From here, I write, coach leaders and travel on weekends to preach. It doesn't feel like home yet—I'm not sure anywhere does right now—but it is a very sweet stopping-point along the trail.

I write these final words from a hospital room. Once again I sit in an outpatient chair with an IV in my arm. I'm disappointed that I've not yet reached a place of health where I can be done with this treatment. At the same time, I'm very grateful that it is available.

Having an IV in my arm as I bring this book to a close feels oddly "right." Some might call it "poetic." Between the comings and goings of friendly nurses, I once again have time to reflect. I feel prompted to open my Bible to Isaiah. The prophet's words provide the basis for a fitting closure for this collection of reflections I've shared with you.

PASSING THROUGH

"When you pass through the waters, I will be with you; and when you pass through the rivers, they will not sweep over you. When you walk through the fire, you will not be burned; the flames will not set you ablaze" (Isaiah 43:2).

If you listen to some forms of Christianity today, you'd be convinced that if you just do the right things, believe the right things or have enough faith, you'll never have problems. You've heard this message, haven't you? It comes subtly, but it comes powerfully.

It is so powerful that when trials do come into our lives we get angry with God. *But God, I don't deserve this. I was doing everything right!* And, before we know it, we've convinced ourselves that God is at fault. He has failed us. A cosmic injustice has occurred, and we are the victim.

We seem to view faith as a security fence designed to keep out of our yard all of the things that we fear.

Perhaps our views aren't serving us well. Perhaps our views aren't even biblical. I've been happy to discover that the Scripture presents a far richer truth.

When you carefully read passages like this from Isaiah, you realize that God is not promising us that we'll never have difficulties. In fact, the premise of the verse is that we *will* have difficulties. Christians today seem stunned, *Hey, what am I doing in this flood? How did I end up here? What went wrong? I'm walking through a fire right now! What happened?*

Peter will tell us later in Scripture, "Do not be surprised at the fiery ordeal that has come on to test you, as though something strange were happening to you" (1 Peter 4:12). No shock here. No surprise.

Jesus says it so clearly, I don't know how we miss it: "In this world you will have trouble" (John 16:33).

The assumption of God's spokespersons throughout the Scriptures is that hardship is part of our earthly existence. Yet, the joyful declaration is that hardship isn't the whole story! The things we dread may prowl about, but rather than truly harming us, they serve as an opportunity for God to reveal Himself more fully to us. This is the repeated assurance of God's Word.

- The waters may rise, but God walks with us through the flood. (Isaiah 43:2)

- The flames may burn around us, but they need not harm us. (Isaiah 43:2)

- Any suffering we experience actually serves to connect us more intimately with the suffering Christ. (1 Peter 4:13, Philippians 3:10)

- We take heart in our trials, knowing that we serve the Overcomer Himself! (John 16:33)

I don't like floods and fires, trials and tribulations any more than you do. But, having a few years of experience with them now, I do want to testify to the goodness of God in the midst of the darkness of life.

The Hebrew language has a variety of words for "darkness." One such word carries the idea of *gloom* and comes from the word for *mourning*. Another word describes the *thick darkness* of a heavy cloud. The word that intrigues me most is the one often used by the prophet Isaiah. More than a dozen times he refers to a type of darkness that carries with it the idea of a *secret place, obscurity*. The word's root means "to grow dim or dark, to hide."

"Let the one who walks in the dark [obscure, hidden places], who has no light, trust in the name of the LORD and rely on their God" (Isaiah 50:10).

David used the same word in the much-loved 139th Psalm: "If I say, 'Surely the darkness will hide me and the light become night around me,' even the darkness will not be dark to you; the night will shine like the day, for darkness is as light to you."

I rejoice in the fact that our God is the God of the day *and* the night, the light *and* the darkness. In fact, the same Hebrew word is used in Isaiah as God declares, "I form the light and create darkness" (45:7). Evidently, He's the God who is complex enough to use and even create the obscuring darkness. He even promises, "I will give you the treasures of darkness, riches stored in secret places" (Isaiah 45:3, NIV 1984).

This is more than a word study for me. This is my recent life story. In the obscurity of recovery from a life-threatening illness, in the isolation of those long, long months, I came to discover that there were treasures waiting in the dark.

Fires and floods, trials and tribulations do come, but they do not come without His grace. Nor do they come to stay. We're just passing through.

Someone thanked me recently for sharing "my" story with them. I laughed in response and said, "Well, I don't really feel like it's 'my' story. If I was choosing 'my' story, I wouldn't have picked this one!"

But, it is the story that I have the privilege to live. By reading these pages you've "lived it" with me. Thank you. If you've been encouraged or strengthened in any way as a result, that encourages and strengthens me as well.

On the trail with you,
John Stumbo

EPILOGUE

I believed my manuscript was done. Relieved, I slipped into bed and peacefully drifted off to sleep. At 2:30 a.m. I awakened, realizing that this book needed one final word. I made my way through the dark and turned on a small desk light so as not to disturb Joanna. On a piece of scratch paper, I scribbled the following:

I have to wonder if someone is coming to the end of this book thinking, "It's great you experienced a miracle, John. But, I haven't. I'm still very much 'in the midst' of my crisis. Do you have a word for me?"

Yes.

God—the Great Artist—is writing a unique story in your life. We can learn from each other, but each life has its own story line. And, each story will be better with God as the main character of every chapter.

In other words, keep trusting . . . not throwing your hope solely upon what God will do for you, but on who He is. He is good and He is in your journey. He may not act as—or when—you'd expect, but He has not abandoned you, nor will He ever leave you.

In fact, the Master Craftsman is up to something very beautiful in your life. The Potter's methods may seem harsh sometimes . . . the Artist's palate too dark. The Author's topic is not one we would have chosen.

Yet, His hands continue to shape, paint and write. The pot's not fully formed. The portrait's not finished. The story has more chapters. He's not done.

Do we not want His plot, His hues, His craftsmanship? Do we really want to write our own stories, paint a self portrait and shape our own lives? Is this not what it is to be a Christ-follower—to yield ourselves into His hand?

I cannot give you answers to all your questions, but I can give you the assurance that the One who began the good work in you will carry it on to completion until the day of Christ's return (see Philippians 1:6).

Another day dawns. I enter my scribbles into my laptop. As I do, I'm eager for you to receive this final word of encouragement from me. It comes with my prayers for you: prayers for strength, courage and hope. They are not just hollow words. They are real. They are available.

Please know this: As long as you have God, you have hope. With hope comes courage and with courage, strength. God will not leave you indefinitely in your current crisis. He will change our situation, or He will change you in the midst of the situation . . . or both. Keep clinging to Him. You are not stuck, trapped or doomed. Never.

Instead, you are loved, held and cherished. Always.

It is true: As long as we have God, we have hope . . . and, we will *always* have God.

———

*To him who is able to keep you from stumbling
and to present you before his glorious presence
without fault and with great joy—
to the only God our Savior be
glory, majesty, power and authority,
through Jesus Christ our Lord,
before all ages,
now and forevermore!
Amen.*

Jude 24–25

For John's speaking itinerary,
book information and other resources
please visit johnstumbo.com.
You can also follow John on
Twitter @John_Stumbo_CMA